CITIZENS OF THE HEAVENLY CITY

A CATECHISM OF CATHOLIC SOCIAL TEACHING

BY

ARTHUR M. HIPPLER

BORROMEO BOOKS
ST. PAUL, MINNESOTA
Additional offices in:
ROCKFORD, ILLINOIS

Imprimatur

+Raymond L. Burke

Bishop of La Crosse, Wisconsin

November 23, 2003

Borromeo Books

PO Box 7273

St. Paul, MN 55107

ISBN: 0-9763098-2-3

Cover design by Chris Wetton

Interior design by George A. Kendall

Printed in the United States of America, 2005

TABLE OF CONTENTS

Foreword

In his Apostolic Letter, "At the Close of the Great Jubilee of the Year 2000," *Novo millennio ineunte,* His Holiness, Pope John Paul II, sets forth the pastoral program of the Church at the beginning of a new Christian millennium (Pope John Paul II, Apostolic Letter, "At the Close of the Great Jubilee of the Year 2000," *Novo millennio ineunte,* no. 29). The Apostolic Letter, addressed to the universal Church, is the occasion for every member of Christ's faithful to examine anew the integrity of his or her living in Christ, so that the life of the Church may be marked by the new enthusiasm and energy required for our time and so often urged with us by our Holy Father.

His Holiness makes clear that the pastoral program of the Church at this time is, in essence, what it has always been: it is Christ Himself, the Gospel, and the living Tradition of the Church articulated in her Magisterium (*ibid,* no.31). The pastoral program of the Church, namely, Christ alive for us in the Church, is expressed in the life of each of the faithful by that Christ-likeness which we call holiness. It is reflected in the daily conversion of life, by which we strive to meet, in the words of our Holy Father, "the high standard of ordinary Christian living" (*ibid*).

In order to carry out the mission of the Church, namely, to proclaim Christ to the world in our time, certain pastoral priorities must be understood and observed. Our Holy Father lists them for us: after holiness of life itself comes prayer and participation in the life of the Sacraments, especially the Holy Eucharist and the Sacrament of Penance; study of the Word of God, as it is faithfully presented in the Church's teaching; and, lastly, proclamation of the Word of God through witness to Christ in the world, which is exemplified, above all, in the heroic virtue of the saints, especially the holy martyrs.

It is in the context of the new evangelization, that is, the context of the pastoral program set forth for us by our Holy Father, that I am honored to present to you *Citizens of the Heavenly City*, by Dr. Arthur M. Hippler. *Citizens of the Heavenly City* is directed to helping our youth to carry out the pastoral program of the Church in their lives, especially to helping them to understand and to observe the pastoral priority of witnessing to Christ in their ordinary Christian living. It is a text which will also be fruitfully studied by adults who desire to deepen their own understanding of what it means to live in Christ in the context of the family and of society, both the neighborhood and the world.

Among the many merits of Dr. Hippler's textbook is the attention to the totality of the Church's social teaching, beginning with the sources of the Church's moral teaching and then progressing to a study of the social implications of the love of God and the love of neighbor. True to what our Holy Father sets forth for us in *Novo millennio ineunte*, which is the perennial teaching of the Church, Dr. Hippler sets his presentation of the Church's social teaching in the context of the Kingship of Our Lord Jesus Christ Who reigns in the world through the piercing of His Most Sacred Heart out of love for all.

Consistent with the presentation of the Church's social teaching as a response to the rich mercy of God toward us, represented in the Sacred Heart of Jesus, Dr. Hippler helps us to understand the individual tenets of the Church's social teaching by guiding us through the Magisterium of the Church, which has never failed to address the Word of Christ to the situation of man in the world. Through the study of Dr. Hippler's textbook, young people and other faithful will grow in familiarity with those texts of the Church's Magisterium which are critical for the transformation of our society into a civilization of divine love.

In presenting Dr. Hippler's textbook to you, I urge you to study it with care. Most of all, I urge you to join to your study of the Catholic Church's social teaching a life of prayer and worship, and to follow up your study of Dr. Hippler's textbook by your daily efforts to witness faithfully to Christ by meeting what is indeed "the high standard of ordinary Christian living."

May God grant that, through the study of *Citizens of the Heavenly City*, we may all grow in our knowledge and love of Christ, and witness to Him faithfully in the world.

+MOST REV. RAYMOND LEO BURKE

BISHOP OF LA CROSSE

CITIZENS
OF THE
HEAVENLY CITY

Introduction:
Individual Rights versus Moral Perfection

From an early age, our society teaches us to celebrate the rights of the individual. Our *Declaration of Independence* proclaims that we are endowed with "unalienable Rights, among which are Life, Liberty and the pursuit of Happiness." It is only natural then that, when we think of society, we think of it as a means for protecting and promoting people's "rights." By *right* I mean a claim that one can make upon others, a claim which they have a duty to fulfill. When I say that I have a "right to life," that means I have a claim on other people not to kill me.

But does this way of looking at society fit with the teachings of God in His divine law? Read the Ten Commandments: "Do not kill, do not commit adultery, do not steal," etc. There is no word that could be safely translated as "right" in our sense. Look at the two commandments of love: "Love God with your whole heart, your whole soul, and your whole strength, and your neighbor as yourself." Jesus does not proclaim that we have "rights" in the modern sense. While Catholics may address social issues using the word "rights," Catholic social teaching, going back to the Ten Commandments, has no need for this term.

The divine law tells us what duties we have to God. And because we owe obedience to God, we also have certain duties to our neighbor. While many people will speak of "rights" as if they differ from morality, Catholics understand our duties to God and neighbor as moral obligations for our own good and that of the community.

What do we mean by the word "good?" We use this word in several ways. We may mean by good that something is *useful*. That is, money is good because we can use it to buy things that we need. We may mean by the word good that something is *pleasant* or *fun*. For example, we call movies or some entertainment good because we enjoy them. Finally, we call something good when it *perfects us in some way*. That is, health is good because it perfects the body. A healthy body acts the way it should. Similarly, knowledge is a good of the mind. The mind is meant to know, and a mind without knowledge is like a body without health. That is why no one wants to be sick, and no one wants to be ignorant.

Because this book is concerned not only with individuals but also with society, we will speak frequently of the *common good*. The common good is not the good of a particular person, but rather the good of a community, whether that community is as small as a family or as big as a nation (*Catechism of the Catholic Church* [hereafter referred to as *CCC*], nos. 1905-1906).

St. Augustine described the common good as one "which is not diminished by being shared with others" (*On Christian Doctrine*, Book I, 1). Hence, we can define the common good in the following way: *a common good is a good that can be shared in by all, and does not diminish when it is divided.* Money or food, for example, cannot be common goods. The more people that try to share in them, the smaller the portion that each receives. Peace however is a common good. When a family or a city has peace, the peace does not get smaller for each. Rather, the more people share in the peace, the more peace there is.

All law is ordered to the common good. When we make laws, we do not have in mind the good of individuals, but the good of the whole community (*CCC*, no.1898). Not only is this true of the laws we make in our states and countries, but it is also true of the laws that come to us from God. But God is directing us to a good beyond the earthly good of our own country. He is directing us to Himself, for He is the most universal common good. In the heavenly city, we share in God's goodness, and no one's share in that goodness takes away from another's.

In this book, we will examine the most basic precepts of Catholic social teaching as they flow from the Ten Commandments of the Old Law and the Two Commandments of the New Law. We will explain each part using the Bible, the Church Fathers and Doctors, and the Popes, especially those of the modern age. The better we understand our teaching, the better we are able to live it, and to act for our true happiness.

Do not be surprised if you find that many of our beliefs as Catholics about morality and politics conflict with the opinions of the society around you. A *secularized* society, that is, a society that does not make God the center of all things, is bound to teach a completely different doctrine about human happiness. Do not even be surprised if many Catholics do not fully understand their own beliefs! Since Catholics live in a secularized society, they are surrounded by many who discourage them from living their faith. We must always pray for conversion of those who do not have the fullness of faith, and at the same time, pray that we grow in the faith despite the many obstacles our society puts before us.

We will examine the Ten Commandments of the Old Law, keeping in mind the Two Commandments of the New Law. The Ten Commandments themselves have two parts: the first part or table of the law addresses our duties to Almighty God; the second part or table of the law addresses our duties to our neighbor.

Why do both the Old Law and New Law put God first? God is our Creator and final happiness. He made us, provides for us, and directs us back to Himself. Everything in the universe is for His sake. If you look at an army, all the parts of the army work together under the direction of the general. The general in turn directs the army to its final goal, victory. Likewise, all the parts of the universe are ordered finally to God, who is the highest good (*CCC*, no.2052). We too find our completion in God. Hence, the divine law makes clear that God comes first above all.

John Henry Cardinal Newman was born in 1801 and died in 1890. Newman was a minister in the Church of England, who, after long study and interior struggle, entered the Catholic Church in 1845. He was made a cardinal by Pope Leo XIII at the age of 78. Newman addressed many subjects within Church teaching, but he is frequently cited for his teaching on moral conscience. He reminded Christians that a man's conscience must be formed in obedience to the law of God. As he declared, "Conscience has its rights because it has duties," that is, duties that arise from the precepts of the moral law. Everyone must allow his conscience to be formed by the Church so that he will judge rightly what he must do.

Questions for Review

1) Why do we as Americans speak so frequently of our "rights"?

2) When God directs His people in His law, what does He lay down instead of "rights"?

3) What are the different meanings of the word "good"? Which meaning is most important for us in this study?

4) What is the common good? What is an example of the common good?

5) What are the problems of living in a "secularized" society?

Lesson One:
Sources of Catholic Social Teaching

Where do we find the social teaching of the Church? It is common to describe Catholic social teaching as beginning with the encyclical letter of Leo XIII, *Rerum novarum*, in 1891. (An *encyclical* or "circular letter" is a letter of the Pope, usually written to give instruction and direction to the whole Church.) *Rerum novarum* had great importance because it was the Catholic response to the social crisis of the modern world. But Catholic social teaching is as old as revelation itself. God has always taught men how to live together in loving service to Him, which of course is the heart of Catholic social teaching.

The first source of Catholic social teaching is the Bible. In the Old Testament, God chooses the Hebrew people as His own, and reveals the Divine Law to them. Through the law, He teaches the Hebrews not only how to worship and reverence Him, but also how to live rightly in their families and society. The most basic part of this revelation is the Ten Commandments, which still forms the foundation of Catholic moral teaching.

Even though Our Lord perfects the old law in the New Testament, He makes it clear that He is not abolishing it. The New Testament understands the old law in a deeper way, namely in light of the two commandments of love: "Thou shalt love the Lord thy God with thy whole heart and with thy whole soul and with thy whole mind. This is the greatest and the first commandment. And the second is like to this: Thou shalt love thy neighbor as thyself" (*Matt.* 22:37-39). This catechism then will follow the Ten Commandments in explaining Catholic social teaching (cf. *CCC*, nos.2064-2068).

The second source of Catholic social teaching is the Fathers and Doctors of the Church. The Fathers are the first theologians of the Church, who took the teachings of the Apostles and explained and defended them to the Christians of the first centuries. Probably the best known Father we will cite is St. Augustine (354-430), who was the Bishop of Hippo in north Africa. His book *The City of God* is a treasury of teaching on man and society.

All Church Fathers are also called Doctors, that is, "teachers" of the Church, insofar as the Church has taken something from their teaching as her own. But while all Fathers are Doctors, not all Doctors of the Church are Fathers. Many important contributions were made to Church teaching by theologians who lived after the time of the Fathers (c.800). Most famous among the Doctors is St. Thomas Aquinas (1225-1274), who taught at the University of Paris. St. Thomas wrote a vast work called the *Summa Theologiae*, which means the "Summary of Theology." By far, the largest section of the *Summa* is dedicated to moral theology, and it provides many teachings relevant to man's social life.

The third source of Catholic social teaching is the encyclical letters and speeches of the Popes. The writings of the Sovereign Pontiffs in the last two centuries have taken the principles and teachings of the Scriptures, Fathers and Doctors, and applied them to the problems of the modern age. Our Lord while present on earth promised that He would not leave us orphans, that He would continue to direct His people from age to age. The Pope as the Vicar of Christ continues Our Lord's teaching on earth in fulfillment of His promise.

The teaching of the Popes is hardest for us to appreciate, because it is easy to fall into the error of thinking that their teaching applies only to Catholics. We know that while many Christians recognize the authority of Scripture, and many of them respect the Fathers of the Church, only Catholics follow the Pope. The fact that many disregard the Pope's authority does not take away the authority itself. As the Vicar of Christ, the Pope is called to teach all men, not just those who bear the name "Catholic." Even in His own time, not everyone heeded the teaching of Our Lord. Yet this in no way lessened His divine authority.

Another common error is the belief that Popes are rather like American presidents or some other elected official, and thus the governance and teaching of one may be completely unlike the governance and teaching of another. Certainly, different Popes may have different priorities and policies. But Popes are not of different "parties" with different political views. They are united fundamentally in protecting and defending what they have received through the Catholic tradition. A new pope, in other words, does not create a new teaching, but on the whole expresses the same teaching in a new way concerning new problems.

A third error, similar to the second, is that the Popes of the past, say the 19th century, have nothing to say to us in the 21st century, and that the only Pope who matters is the present one. This view is shown false by the writings of the Popes themselves, who continue to refer to their predecessors, and build their explanations on those of past pontiffs. In *Centesimus annus*, for example, Pope John Paul II builds on the teaching of Pope Leo XIII (*Rerum novarum*) and Pope Pius XI (*Quadragesimo anno*). Pope John Paul II frequently uses phrases such as *social justice* and *solidarity*, phrases he does not define, because he assumes the definitions from the writings of Pope Pius XI (*Divini Redemptoris*, no.51) and Pope Pius XII (*Summi pontificatus*, no.35). We have much to learn from the Popes of the past, even though it may seem that their times were very different from ours.

Even though we may enjoy a way of life that is much healthier and more prosperous than earlier ages, human nature is the same in every age. That we are made by God, and called to return to Him in eternal life, is no less true now than it was in the time that Our Lord walked the earth. And that we are weakened, even rebellious, by our fallen human nature against the mercy of God, sadly, is still true as well. In other words, the change in our *material* condition has not changed our *spiritual* condition. And it is to these unchanging spiritual realities that the Popes are constantly drawing our attention, no less in their social teaching than elsewhere.

The Popes have continued to defend the necessity of Christ and the Church He founded. It is true that the Church does not have as its business the invention of new machines or civic codes for the betterment of earthly life, nor does the Church claim this as

Her mission. Rather, the Church works for the sanctification of souls by grace so that, when men die, they go to heaven. All the earthly improvement in the world will not prevent the final end of mortal men, who must die and be judged.

Moses gave the Old Law to the Hebrews after he led them out of Egypt, a law which he received from God Himself. Just as the human law is ordered to creating friendship between man and his neighbors, so the divine law is ordered to create friendship between man and God. Although parts of the Old Law are peculiar to the Hebrew people, the moral commandments of the Old Law, which we call the "Ten Commandments," are shared by many people around the world and throughout history. This should come as no surprise – no society can live in peace that allows murder, theft or lying for its people, even if it tolerates these evils in a few cases. The widespread consent on the moral law shows that the "Ten Commandments" are based on human nature, which is the same everywhere.

11

Questions for Review

1) What is a papal encyclical? Why is *Rerum novarum* considered important for Catholic social teaching?

2) How does the Old Testament contribute to Catholic social teaching? How does the New Testament contribute to Catholic social teaching?

3) What is the difference between a Church Father and a Church Doctor? What are the contributions of the Fathers and the Doctors to Catholic social teaching?

4) Why do we study the writings of the Popes? Are the writings of the Popes addressed only to Catholics?

5) Why are the differences between Popes unlike the differences of secular leaders, such as the President of United States?

6) Why is it that the Popes of ages long ago still have teaching that should be important for us today?

Lesson Two:

Kingship of Jesus Christ

Every year on the last Sunday of November, the Church observes the Solemnity of Christ the King. This feast was instituted by Pope Pius XI in 1925. At that time, Europe was still recovering from the bloodshed and destruction of the First World War (1914-1918). Why, the Pope asked, were people killing each other as never before? Why were nations and peoples within nations not working effectively for peace? Pius XI blamed it on one thing — the rejection of the kingship of Jesus Christ:

> ...As long as individuals and states refused to submit to the rule of Our Savior, there would be no really hopeful prospect of a lasting peace among nations (*Quas primas*, no.1).

We may think of Jesus in many ways — as our savior, as our teacher, as our brother in His humanity. But we often forget that He is a king. In a democracy, most of our rulers are elected. We choose our governors, our senators, our presidents, and so on. We may think of a king as someone foreign, or historical. But Jesus was, is, and ever shall be the King of all Humanity!

The Prophets of Israel foretold the coming of a Messiah or an "Anointed One" who would be a king. David speaks in the person of the Messiah in his Psalms when he sings:

> But I am appointed king by him over Sion, his holy moun-
> tain, preaching his commandment. The Lord hath said to
> me: Thou art my son, this day have I begotten thee. Ask of
> me, and I will give thee the Gentiles for thy inheritance, and
> the utmost parts of the earth for thy possession (*Ps.* 2:6-8).

The Prophet Isaiah foretold that the Messiah would be a Prince
of Peace. We often hear this passage around the Christmas sea-
son:

> For a CHILD IS BORN to us, and a son is given to us, and
> the government is upon his shoulder: and his name shall be
> called, Wonderful, Counsellor, God the Mighty, the Father
> of the world to come, the Prince of Peace. His empire shall
> be multiplied, and there shall be no end of peace: he shall sit
> upon the throne of David, and upon his kingdom; to estab-
> lish it and strengthen it with judgment and with justice,
> from henceforth and for ever: the zeal of the Lord of hosts
> will perform this (*Is.* 9:6-7).

The Prophet Zacharias foretold that the Messiah would come as
a king, but in humble appearance. This prophecy was fulfilled
when Jesus entered Jerusalem on a donkey:

> Rejoice greatly, O daughter of Sion, shout for joy, O daugh-
> ter of Jerusalem: BEHOLD THY KING will come to thee,
> the just and saviour: he is poor, and riding upon an ass, and
> upon a colt the foal of an ass (*Zac.* 9:9; see also *Matt.* 21:5).

Through Mary, Jesus was descended from King David. So in His humanity, He was of royal blood. In the Gospel of Luke, we are told that

> He shall be great and shall be called the Son of the Most High. And the Lord God shall give unto him the throne of David his father: and he shall reign in the house of Jacob for ever. And of his kingdom there shall be no end (*Luke* 1:32-33).

Jesus refers to Himself as a king, especially at the last judgment:

> And when the Son of man shall come in his majesty, and all the angels with him, then shall he sit upon the seat of his majesty. And all nations shall be gathered together before him: and he shall separate them one from another, as the shepherd separateth the sheep from the goats (*Matt.* 25:31-32).

These passages make it clear that Jesus is a king. But it is fair to ask: maybe Jesus is king of the Jews, because He is descended from David — but what makes Him king over all humanity?

Jesus is king for two reasons. First, Jesus is both God and man. His Divinity gives Him authority over us, for He too, with the Father and the Holy Spirit, is Our Creator. He is a king by His divine nature. Second, He is Our Savior. By His sacrifice on the cross at Calvary, He won back our souls from the Devil. So He is also a king by conquering the enemy of our souls.

CITIZENS OF THE HEAVENLY CITY

We may think that Christ's kingship over us is entirely personal. But Scripture and Tradition teach us that Jesus must not only be the king of individual souls, but of families, cities and nations (*CCC*, no.2105). Jesus does not want to be the ruler only of hearts in a private way. As Creator and Savior of all mankind, He deserves the obedience of everyone! All rulers must have Jesus as their superior, or else they will rule unjustly. Society must have Jesus as its king, or else it will suffer.

The Bible shows that religion is not merely a "private matter" between man and God. When God chose the Hebrews as His People, He gave them His Law, and taught them how to worship Him and live in holiness. For example, the Passover feast was observed by the whole people at a certain time every year. He did not leave them to choose their own way of worship and morality.

Similarly, on the night before He was betrayed, Our Lord took the Passover feast and transformed it into a memorial of His Passion by which we were redeemed. Our Lord instructed His priests about what to say and how to say it. And all Christians are called to participate in the ritual He instituted, which we call the Sacrifice of the Mass. Both in the Old Testament and the New, we are called as a people to worship and follow God in a common way, not just privately as individuals.

The Scriptures also show that, just as the Hebrews were called to obey as a people, they were often rewarded or punished as a people. When they obeyed God, their lives were good and happy. They lived at peace and enjoyed prosperity. But when they failed to follow God's law, they suffered immensely, often by such calamities as famine or invasion.

> That thou mayst love the Lord thy God, and walk in his ways, and keep his commandments and ceremonies and judgments, and bless thee in the land, which thou shalt go in to possess. But if thy heart be turned away, so that thou wilt not hear, and being deceived with error thou adore strange gods, and serve them: I foretell thee this day that thou shalt perish, and shalt remain but a short time in the land, to which thou shalt pass over the Jordan, and shalt go in to possess it (*Deut.* 30:16-18).

So we also suffer when we reject the Kingship of Jesus Christ. While we are ultimately judged as individuals, our salvation or damnation happens as a part of a community, whether the secular community or that of the Church.

We may think that because other nations have different religious beliefs, that Jesus should not be king of all humanity. How can Jesus be King of Buddhists or Jews? But in fact Jesus is the true king of all humanity, whether people recognize Him or not. Pope Leo XIII tells us:

> His Empire includes not only Catholic nations, not only baptized persons who, though of right belonging to the Church, have been led astray by error, or have been cut off from her by schism, but also all those who are outside the

Christian faith; so that truly the whole of mankind is subject to the power of Jesus Christ (*Annum sacrum,* no.3).

If some group in Montana said that they did not recognize the President's authority, and that they were going to elect their own president, we would see immediately that this would not change the real president of the United States. Similarly, just because people deny that Jesus is our Creator and Savior, does not for a moment change the fact that He is truly our Creator and our Savior, and that all men owe Him their obedience.

When we pray the Our Father, we pray "Thy kingdom come." We pray for the coming of the kingdom, meaning the rule of Jesus over all peoples of the world. We pray that all might be brought under His loving authority. The Kingship of Christ is the first goal for all Catholic social action, for Christ must reign! (*I Cor* 15:25).

Blessed Miguel Pro was a young Jesuit priest, executed during the persecution of Catholics by the Mexican government in 1927. Although we think of Latin American countries as deeply Catholic, many have suffered revolutions that brought anti-Catholic, even anti-religious governments to power. In Mexico, Catholic schools were closed, religious orders of priests and nuns expelled and churches confiscated or

destroyed. Blessed Miguel spread out his hands in the form of a cross before his execution, crying out "Viva Cristo Rey!" which means "Long live Christ the King!" He was beatified by Pope John Paul II on Sept. 5, 1988.

Questions for Review

1) Why did Pope Pius XI institute the Feast of Christ the King?

2) How do the Scriptures of the Old Testament show that the Messiah would be a king?

3) How is this kingship fulfilled in Jesus Christ?

4) Why is religion not merely a private or personal matter, but public and social? How do we see this in the Old Testament?

5) Why do all people owe obedience to Jesus Christ, even if they are not Christian?

Lesson Three:
True Worship and Society

In the first commandment, God decrees, "Thou shalt not have strange gods before me. Thou shalt not make to thyself *a graven thing, nor the likeness of any thing* that is in heaven above, or in the earth beneath, nor of those things that are in the waters under the earth. Thou shalt not adore them, nor serve them" (*Ex.* 20:3-5). God reveals Himself to the Hebrew people as the only true God, and therefore the only God worthy of our reverence: "Thou shalt fear the Lord thy God, and shalt serve him only, and thou shalt swear by his name" (*Deut.* 6:13).

What does it mean to "worship God"? We may think of going to church as worship; but before Christ, there were no churches. How did they worship?

All over the world, people worship through sacrifice. For example, if you read the epic poems of Homer, the *Iliad* and the *Odyssey,* you will see that the ancient Greeks sacrificed oxen and sheep to their gods. The ancient Egyptians sacrificed birds. The purpose of the sacrifice is the same; by "offering up" a prized possession, one makes a visible sign of submission to the divine authority. It is not enough to worship silently in our hearts. For our thoughts to be known and shared, they must be expressed in words and actions. Sacrifice is the action that allows our reverence for God to be known and shared with others.

After Adam's fall, men remembered that they should offer sacrifice to God. One sees this with Cain and Abel (*Gen.* 4:3-4). But after many generations, they began to worship gods of their own creation. When we worship a false god that we have made up ourselves, this is the sin of *idolatry.* Instead of offering sacrifice to the true God, men offered sacrifice to idols, or imitations of God. This is the how the Greeks and the Egyptians ended up sacrificing to their "gods" instead of God Almighty.

When God gave the Law to the Hebrews through Moses, He taught them how He wished to be worshipped. And the central act of this worship was sacrifice. Through this, God had two purposes. First, He wished the Hebrews to honor Him as the Creator of the universe, as the source of all life. As David says, "...all things are thine: and we have given thee what we received of thy hand" (*1Par.* 29:14 [*1 Chron.-NAB*]). Second, by teaching them right worship, they would avoid falling into idolatry, which He condemned in the strongest way: "He that sacrificeth to gods, shall be put to death, save only to the Lord" (*Ex.* 22:20).

As often as the people worshipped God in the right way, they lived in peace and prosperity. But we read time and time again of how they turned away from God, and fell into the idolatry of the peoples who lived around them. For this, God punished them with invasion and bloodshed:

> And [they] served their idols, and it became a stumblingblock to them. And they sacrificed their sons, and their daughters to devils. And they shed innocent blood: the blood of their sons and of their daughters which they sacri-

ficed to the idols of Chanaan. And the land was polluted with blood, And was defiled with their works: and they went aside after their own inventions. And the Lord was exceedingly angry with his people: and he abhorred his inheritance.

And he delivered them into the hands of the nations: and they that hated them had dominion over them. And their enemies afflicted them: and they were humbled under their hands (*Ps.* 105:36-42 [*Ps.*106-*NAB*]).

In the fullness of time, Jesus Christ was born in fulfillment of the prophecies that predicted a *Messiah* ("Anointed One") who would save His people from their sins: "And she shall bring forth a son: and thou shalt call his name JESUS. For he shall save his people from their sins" (*Matt.* 1:21). He came not only for the Jewish people, but also for all people, Jews and Gentiles. Jesus came to offer Himself as the perfect sacrifice. That is why John the Baptist greeted Him as the "Lamb of God" (*John* 1:29). Just as the Paschal Lamb was sacrificed in the Old Law to save the Hebrews from the Angel of Death, so also in the New Law the blood of Jesus would be offered for man's salvation.

When we attend Holy Mass, we are attending a re-presentation of that same sacrifice, only under the appearances of bread and wine (*CCC*, no.1366). In a mystical and very real sense, we are once again at the cross of Calvary: "In this Eucharistic sacrifice Christ Himself, our Salvation and our Redeemer, immolates Himself each day for all of us and mercifully pours out on us the countless riches of His grace. No blood is shed, but the sacrifice is real, just as real as when Christ hung from a cross of

Calvary" (Pope John XXIII, *Ad Petri cathedram*, no.175). When the priest says the words of consecration, we once more hear the words of Jesus, offering His life on the Cross in atonement for our sins.

In the place of sacrificing creatures that can never make peace between God and us, God has given us His own Son as a sacrifice. As Pope Paul VI explains:

> Just as Moses with the blood of calves had sanctified the Old Testament (*Ex.* 24:8), so also Christ Our Lord, through the institution of the Mystery of the Eucharist, with His own Blood sanctified the New Testament, whose Mediator He is. For, as the Evangelists narrate, at the Last Supper "He took bread, and blessed and broke it, and gave it to them, saying: 'This is My Body, given for you; do this for a commemoration of Me. And so with the cup, when supper was ended. This cup, He said, is the New Testament, in My Blood which is to be shed for you'" (*Luke* 22:19-20, cf. *Matt.* 26:26-28; *Mark* 14:22-24). And by bidding the Apostles to do this in memory of Him, He made clear His will that the same sacrifice be forever repeated   (*Mysterium fidei*, no.29).

Consequently, in worshipping God in the Holy Sacrifice of the Mass, we are worshipping God in the best way. As Leo XIII declares, "Nothing can give greater honor, nothing can be more pleasing to God" than the Eucharistic Sacrifice:

For it is only in virtue of the death that Christ suffered that man can satisfy, and that most abundantly, the demands of God's justice, and can obtain the plenteous gifts of His clemency (*Mirae caritatis,* nos.17-18).

There is no substitute for the perfect sacrifice of Jesus Christ, which is re-presented in the Mass. And just as the people of the Old Testament would turn away from God in idolatry, so people of our time turn away from the true God to false religions, or worse, no religion at all.

Indeed, many countries are guided by the principles of *secularism,* which means that they exclude religion as much as possible from public life. In our country, we believe in a "separation of Church and State." (It is worth noting that this phrase is not found in our Constitution.) This used to mean that the government officially endorses no single denomination to the exclusion of others. Today it seems to mean that no religion in general may be expressed in our political and social life. This secularism is an opinion that the Popes have condemned:

As we are each of us admonished by the very voice of nature to worship God in piety and holiness, as the Giver unto us of life and of all that is good therein, so also and for the same reason, nations and States are bound to worship Him (Leo XIII, *Humanum genus,* no.24).

John Paul II described this secularism as a "culture of death." Although most people think of the culture of death as the acceptance of abortion, euthanasia and any unjust killing, John Paul II tells us:

In seeking the deepest roots of the struggle between the 'culture of life' and the 'culture of death'…We have to go to the heart of the tragedy experienced by modern man: *the eclipse of the sense of God and of man,* typical of a social and cultural climate dominated by secularism, which, with its ubiquitous tentacles, succeeds at times in putting Christian communities to the test *(Evangelium vitae,* no.21).

This "eclipse of the sense of God" is most evident when we fall into the error of thinking that the right worship of God is unnecessary for our society. Just as the Hebrew people suffered when they followed idols, so also we suffer with the evils of our present age when the Sacrifice of the Mass is neglected or despised.

As Catholics, we certainly do not believe that people should be "forced" to worship, that the laws should compel people to religious beliefs which conflict with their own (*CCC*, no.2106). For the sake of the common good, we must tolerate those who do not share our faith. At the same time, we must recognize that the Mass is the one true sacrifice that God has given us to reconcile us with Himself. And the more that unbelievers, through the grace of conversion, come to share in the richness of the Mass, the more abundantly these graces will benefit society.

St. Pius X reigned from 1903 to 1914, and is the only modern Pope who is a canonized saint. Pope St. Pius is best known for his condemnation of "modernism," a religious error that denied the basic dogmas of the faith. This error continues to plague the Church in various forms to the present day. Many believe that the outbreak of the First World War so saddened Pope Pius that he died of a broken heart.

Questions for Review

1) How are worship and sacrifice part of human nature?

2) Why did God give instructions to the Hebrews about worship and sacrifice?

3) How is the death of Jesus on the cross a "sacrifice"?

4) How does the Mass share in the Sacrifice of the Cross?

5) What is "secularism," and why is it wrong?

Lesson Four:
Blasphemy and Free Speech

In the second commandment, our Lord declares, "Thou shalt not take the name of the Lord thy God in vain: for the Lord will not hold him guiltless that shall take the name of the Lord his God in vain" (*Ex.* 20:7). First, we should ask, how is it that we should speak of God? Second, what does it mean to take Our Lord's name in vain?

How should we speak of God's name? In the *Book of Psalms*, David tells us that we must always speak of God with blessing: "Sing ye to the Lord and bless His name" (*Ps.* 95:2 [*Ps.*96-*NAB*]); and praise: "...and my mouth shall praise thee with joyful lips" (*Ps.* 62:6 [*Ps.*63-*NAB*]). Elsewhere, the Psalmist sings:

> Praise the Lord, ye children: praise ye the name of the Lord. Blessed be the name of the Lord, from henceforth now and for ever. From the rising of the sun unto the going down of the same, the name of the Lord is worthy of praise (*Ps.* 112:1-3 [*Ps.*113-*NAB*]).

When we bless and praise the name of God, we are proclaiming God's goodness. We recognize Him as our Creator, our Lord and our Savior. God does not need our praise, but we need to praise God to increase our devotion to Him.

When we fail to give God reverence in our speech, we take His name *in vain,* that is, we use His name for no good purpose. We sin when we use God's name for the sake of expressing our anger, or merely for amusement, or worst of all, to insult God or deny His goodness. When we insult God or things related to Him, this is the sin of blasphemy (*CCC*, no.2148).

Blasphemy is a very grave sin. In the Old Testament, blasphemy was punished by the death penalty: "...the man that curseth his God, shall bear his sin: And he that blasphemeth the name of the Lord, dying let him die..." (*Lev.* 24:15-16). In *Revelation,* blasphemy is punished by divine justice: "And men were scorched with great heat: and they blasphemed the name of God, who hath power over these plagues. Neither did they penance to give him glory" (*Apoc.* 16:9 [*Rev.-NAB*]). When the Pharisees accuse Jesus of working miracles through the power of the Devil, He tells them: "But he that shall blaspheme against the Holy Ghost, shall never have forgiveness, but shall be guilty of an everlasting sin" (*Mark* 3:29).

Blasphemy includes not only bad or false things that are said about God, but also bad or false things said about His Church, the saints, the angels, and other sacred things worthy of our reverence (*CCC*, no.2146). St. Thomas comments that when St. Paul writes in *Ephesians* (4:31), "Let...blasphemy, be put away from you," he includes "that which is committed against God or the saints" (IIaIIae,Q13, art.1, 2nd reply).

In our own time, we do not think that using God's name in vain is a public problem. Many people will attack God and His Church in public ways, on television and in movies. Those who attack the Church will argue that they have a right to their own opinion and the right to "free speech." It is however a sin against justice to slander the innocent. One protects freedom of speech so that people may freely speak about what is just or useful. Pope Leo XIII long ago warned against "free speech" that has no relation to the restraints of virtue:

> If unbridled license of speech and of writing is granted to all, nothing will remain sacred or inviolate; even the highest and truest mandates of natures, justly held to be the common and noble heritage of the human race, will not be spared. Thus, truth being gradually obscured by darkness, pernicious and manifold error, as too often happens, will easily prevail (Leo XIII, *Libertas,* no.23).

When we think of freedom of speech, we must always remember the good for which we protect this privilege. Freedom of speech is evil when it allows harm for others and the common good. No one, for example, thinks that someone has the right to shout "fire!" in a crowded movie theater as a joke. We limit the freedom of speech when it hurts the common good. Free speech without restraint undermines the common good, as Pope Gregory XVI explains:

> Experience shows, even from earliest times, that cities renowned for wealth, dominion, and glory perished as a result of this single evil, namely immoderate freedom of opinion, license of free speech, and desire for novelty (*Mirari vos,* no.14).

Leo XIII makes the same point in the following way:

So, too, the liberty of thinking, and of publishing, whatso-
ever each one likes, without any hindrance, is not in itself
an advantage over which society can wisely rejoice. On the
contrary, it is the fountainhead and origin of many evils.
Liberty is a power perfecting man, and hence should have
truth and goodness for its object. But the character of goodness and truth cannot be changed at option (*Immortale Dei,*
no.32).

If we are truthful, we do not believe that people should be free
to slander the reputation of those who are dear to us. And yet,
many Catholics do not understand the gravity of those who
slander the Church Christ has founded, who, in the words of
Leo XIII "attack with impunity the very foundations of the
Catholic religion, in speech, in writing, and in teaching" (*Humanum genus,* no.14).

Freedom is not an end, worthy in itself. It is a means to finding
the truth, and to loving the good.

Gregory XVI reigned from 1831 to 1846. The effects of the French Revolution and the spread of its secularist political teaching by the armies of Napoleon had weakened the influence of Catholic social teaching in Europe. Pope Gregory wrote *Mirari vos* and *Singulari nos* against the errors of a French priest, Félicité Robert de Lamennais, who taught an exaggerated form of civil liberty that undermined obedience to just authority. While combating the liberal and secularist attacks on Catholicism, Pope Gregory also tried to establish justice and toleration for the Church in countries where it was persecuted by anti-Catholic governments, as in Spain, Poland and France.

Questions for Review

1) What does it mean to take the name of the Lord in vain?

2) What is "blasphemy"?

3) Why cannot "free speech" include the freedom to blaspheme God?

4) How could unrestrained freedom of speech destroy a community?

Lesson Five:
Manual Labor and the Sabbath

The third commandment commands us to "keep holy the Sabbath day." For the Hebrew people, this day was Saturday. The Church moved the Sabbath to Sunday, in honor of Our Lord's Resurrection on that day (*CCC*, no.2175). Let us first consider how this commandment applied in the Old Testament, and then explain how it applies in the New Testament:

> Remember that thou keep holy the sabbath day. Six days shalt thou labour, and shalt do all thy works. But on the seventh day is the sabbath of the Lord thy God: thou shalt do no work on it, thou nor thy son, nor thy daughter, nor thy manservant, nor thy maidservant, nor thy beast, nor the stranger that is within thy gates.

> For in six days the Lord made heaven and earth, and the sea, and all things that are in them, and rested on the seventh day: therefore the Lord blessed the seventh day, and sanctified it (*Ex.* 20:8-11).

God commands the Hebrews to keep holy the Sabbath by freeing themselves from manual work on that day. In general, when we work we are doing something for the good of our body, or for the care of our possessions. For the Hebrews, this meant working in the fields for food, or carrying out household chores.

God commanded them to put aside these activities for one day out of the week, so that they might have a day for prayer, worship and rest.

In other words, God wanted one day for His People that they might turn from the needs of their bodies, and look to the good of their souls. God "worked" for six days, and then rested on the seventh. So also, man works for six days, and, on the seventh, rests in the Lord, turning to Him in praise and thanksgiving (*CCC*, no.2172).

By keeping the Sabbath, the Hebrews not only gave honor to God for the creation of the world, but also for their deliverance from slavery under the Egyptians, as we read in *Deuteronomy*:

> The seventh is the day of the sabbath, that is, the rest of the Lord thy God. Thou shalt not do any work therein, thou nor thy son nor thy daughter, nor thy manservant nor thy maidservant, nor thy ox, nor thy ass, nor any of thy beasts, nor the stranger that is within thy gates: that thy manservant and thy maidservant may rest, even as thyself. Remember that thou also didst serve in Egypt, and the Lord thy God brought thee out from thence with a strong hand, and a stretched out arm. Therefore hath he commanded thee that thou shouldst observe the sabbath day (*Deut.* 5:14-15).

Very few people nowadays take the Sabbath seriously. For them, Sunday is a day like any other for chores and work of any kind. But we must remember the words of the prophets to the Hebrew people when they failed to keep the Sabbath. Jeremiah warned the people of his time:

But if you will not hearken to me, to sanctify the sabbath day, and not to carry burdens, and not to bring them in by the gates of Jerusalem on the sabbath day: I will kindle a fire in the gates thereof, And it shall devour the houses of Jerusalem, and it shall not be quenched (*Jer.* 17:27).

The people did not listen. Israel was invaded by the Babylonians, and the Hebrew people were taken as slaves to Babylon. They lived there as exiles for seventy years.

By the time of Our Lord's preaching, the Jews (perhaps understandably) had become excessive in the enforcement of the Sabbath rest. Hence, Jesus proclaims to the Pharisees, "The sabbath was made for man, and not man for the sabbath" (*Mark* 2:27).

After the Church began to observe the Sabbath on Sunday instead of Saturday, the exact prohibitions on manual work were not defined. Christians were urged to avoid manual work on the Sabbath as much as possible (cf. *Catholic Encyclopedia*, "Sunday"). Around the eighth century, the Church forbade manual work, public buying and selling and meetings of the law courts. While Christians should not fall into the excesses of the Pharisees and multiply restrictions on the Sabbath, Christians should not ignore the prohibitions on manual labor. It is not enough to fulfill the Sunday obligation of attending Mass, and then treat the day as any other day in the week. One must dedicate Sunday to prayer and rest.

In the last hundred years or so, many countries that were once Christian have abandoned respect for the Third Commandment and the restrictions it places on manual labor. These societies exert more and more pressure on people to work on Sunday. We are not speaking here, of course, about those professions which must be carried out every day of the week from necessity, e.g. hospital staff, police, farmers, and so on. We are speaking of those professions that are not carried out on Sunday by such necessity (*CCC*, no.2185). Leo XIII explained that rest on Sunday was not a command that people could freely choose to ignore:

> A man cannot even by his free choice allow himself to be treated in a way inconsistent with his nature, and suffer his soul to be enslaved; for there is no question here of rights belonging to man, but of duties owed to God, which are to be religiously observed. Hence follows necessary cessation from toil and work on Sundays and Holy Days of obligation (Leo XIII, *Rerum novarum,* nos.57-58).

Leo XIII says that the Sunday rest belongs to man's "nature" because by nature we have not only bodies, but also immortal souls. This day of the week is set aside for us to act for the good of our spirit. As Pope Leo says, "Rest combined with religion calls man away from toil and the business of daily life to admonish him to ponder on heavenly goods and pay his just and due homage to the Eternal Deity" *(RN,* no.58). The Sabbath rest, then, is not a man-made custom, but a divine command that allows us in some way to give God His due.

In our present day, Pope John Paul II has reminded us of the obligation to free people from manual labor on the Sabbath:

"[O]ne may ask whether existing laws and practices of industrialized societies effectively ensure in our own day the exercise of the basic right to Sunday rest" (*Centesimus annus,* no.9). Workers, he tells us, have the right to rest, and "this involves a regular weekly rest comprising at least Sunday" (*Laborem exercens,* no.93; cf. *CCC*, no.2188).

St. Justin Martyr (c.100-165) is a Church Father of the East or Greek-speaking part of the Christian world, who died as a martyr in Rome. He was trained as a pagan philosopher, and later converted to the Christian faith. He provides us one of the earlier testimonies of the importance of Sunday for Christians: "Sunday is the day on which we all hold our common assembly, because it is the first day on which God, having wrought a change in the darkness and matter, made the world; and Jesus Christ our Saviour on the same day rose from the dead" (*First Apology,* chap. 67; cf. *CCC*, n.2174).

Questions for Review

1) Why did God command His People to rest on the Sabbath? What happened to them when they disobeyed this commandment?

2) How was this commandment modified in Christian practice?

3) What respect do people have for this commandment today?

4) Why is forcing people to work on the Sabbath an injustice, even when they do so voluntarily?

Lesson Six:
Protection of Parental Authority

In the fourth commandment, God says "Honour thy father and thy mother, that thou mayest be long-lived upon the land which the Lord thy God will give thee" (*Ex.* 20:12). This is the first command God gives us that directs us to our neighbor. Why are parents the first "neighbors" to whom we are directed?

All parents are in some way like God Himself, since they provide life and discipline for their children. If we do not honor and obey our parents here on earth, how can we honor and obey God, the supreme parent, who is spiritual and invisible?

But children are not the only ones who must respect parental authority. Civil government as well must respect the just rule of parents over their children. If the parents were to treat their children in a brutal or negligent way, the civil authorities have the duty to protect the children from serious harm, just as they have the duty to protect all innocent people from injustice. Outside of some emergency of this kind, the state cannot absorb the power of parents for itself. By natural justice, children are under the rule of their parents, as St. Thomas explains:

> For a child is by nature part of its father: thus, at first, it is not distinct from its parents as to its body, so long as it is enfolded within its mother's womb; and later on after birth, and before it has the use of its free-will, it is enfolded in the

41

care of its parents, which is like a spiritual womb,...so by natural justice the child, before reaching the use of reason, is under the father's care. Hence it would be contrary to natural justice if the child were removed from the care of its parents, or if any disposition were made concerning him against the will of the parents (*Summa Theologiae, IIaIIae* Q.10, a.12).

In the 19th century, the Socialists proposed that the care of children belonged primarily to the state. The state would decide how children should be raised, where they should go to school, even what they should believe. The civil authorities could contradict parental decisions for their children. In extreme cases, the state could simply remove children from the home, and raise them under government "foster care."

God Himself delegates power to parents over their children. This demands obedience on the part of children, for insofar as parents raise their children according to the moral and divine law, they are expressing the will of God. And as we have seen, governments must in their own way respect parental authority. It cannot be taken away for light and casual reasons, but only for grave abuses on the part of parents.

Pope Leo XIII argued against the Socialists by reaffirming the principle laid down by St. Thomas:

Paternal authority can neither be abolished by the State nor absorbed; for it has the same source as human life itself.

'Children are in some way part of the father,' and as it were, the continuation of the father's personality. Strictly speaking, the child takes its place in civil society not in its own right, but in its quality as a member of the family in which it is begotten. And it is precisely because "the child belongs to the father," that "before it attains the use of free will, it is in the power and care of its parents" (*Summa Theologiae, IIaIIae,* Q.10, a.12, quoted above). The Socialists, therefore, in setting aside the parent and introducing the providence of the State, act against natural justice, and threaten the very existence of family life (*Rerum novarum,* no.14).

Likewise, when Pope Pius XI condemned the errors of the Communists, he included the belief that the mother should be removed from the home so that the "collective" or local government could raise the children. Further, the Communists violated justice by forcing children into government schools against the wishes of their parents. But no one in justice can deprive parents of the power to oversee the education of their own children (*CCC,* no.2229). In the words of Pope Pius XI:

The family, therefore, holds directly from the Creator the mission and hence the right to educate the offspring, a right inalienable because inseparably joined to the strict obligation, a right prior to any right whatever of civil society and of the State, and therefore, inviolable on the part of any power on earth (*Divini Illius Magistri,* no.32).

Consequently, the Popes have always taught that the state must respect the right of parents to have their children educated according to the judgments of their conscience. The Second Vatican Council declared "the public power, which has the obligation to protect and defend the rights of citizens, must see to it, in its concern for distributive justice, that public subsidies are paid out in such a way that parents are truly free to choose according to their conscience the schools they want for their children" (*Gravissimum educationis*, no.6§1). This means that the government has the obligation to support religious schools in accord with the conscience of religious parents.

This is hard for many Americans to accept, because we tend to believe that the government should not support anything religious. This practice forces Catholic parents who support Catholic schools to pay twice; once through their taxes for secular schools, once through their tuition for the Catholic schools. This excessive financial burden can incline families to act against their conscience in favor of the secular school. Justice demands that parents have access to the education, even religious education, for which they have paid in taxes.

Pope Pius XI in his time lamented that in countries of mixed religious beliefs, "a heavy burden weighs upon Catholics, who...support Catholic schools for their children entirely at their own expense; to this they feel obliged in conscience." Catholic education, he argues, should be "aided from public funds, as distributive justice requires"(*Divini Illius Magistri*, no.82). It is from this principle that Catholics and other Christians have spoken out on the need for vouchers, which would allow them to take their tax money and spend it on schools in accord with their conscience. Tuition tax credits are an example of this principle.

Such programs do not intrude Catholic religion into our public schools against the conscience of unbelievers or nonbelievers. Rather, they allow Catholics, through their taxes, to support Catholic schools, and others to support other kinds of schools as their consciences direct them.

Some might object that, by and large, Catholics have accepted secular education, and hence have no question of conscience. Certainly, the Popes have long recognized that a number of circumstances, physical and financial, may prevent Catholics from availing themselves of Catholic schools, even though the parents are very aware of the dangers of a non-religious education. No Catholic however can maintain in conscience that secular schools in general are wholly acceptable and pose no threat to the souls of the young, an opinion condemned by several popes over the last hundred years.

Pope Leo XIII declared in 1897 that "an education in which religion is altered or non-existent is a very dangerous education" and that "No one should be ready to believe that instruction and piety can be separated with impunity." A school that excludes the faith from its instruction cannot remain "neutral." In ways sometimes obvious, sometimes hidden, such an education promotes the view that God is irrelevant to human life.

As Pope Pius XI explained, when "God and Jesus Christ, as well as His doctrines, were banished from the school...the school became not only secular and non-religious but openly atheistical and anti-religious" (*Ubi arcano,* no.30). The experience of these secularized schools led Pius XI to assert elsewhere that a non-religious school "cannot exist in practice; it is bound to become irreligious" (*Divini Illius Magistri,* no.79).

While we may think that an education that makes morality and religion "extra-curricular" is good enough, Pius XI disagreed: "The school forcibly deprived of the right to teach anything about God or His law could not but fail in its efforts to really educate, that is, to lead children to the practice of virtue, for the school lacked the fundamental principles which underlie the possession of a knowledge of God and the means necessary to strengthen the will in its efforts toward good and in its avoidance of sin" (*UA,* no.30). Without the teaching of God's law and the grace of the sacraments, most children have no defenses against the evil influences of today's world.

The difficulties Catholics face in educating their children, financial or otherwise, should never allow them to accept secular schools easily. Indeed, the Second Vatican Council reaffirmed the responsibility of parents to support Catholic schools: "As for Catholic parents, the Council calls them to mind their duty to entrust their children to Catholic schools, when and where this is possible, to support such schools to the extent of their ability, and to work along with them for the welfare of their children" (*Gravissimum educationis,* no.8).

When the state assists Catholics and other religious peoples to educate their children it benefits not only those families but also society as a whole. The teaching of the popes makes clear that morality cannot be preserved without the teaching of the Faith. As Pope Leo XIII explains, "To organize teaching in such a way as to remove it from all contact with religion is therefore to corrupt the very seeds of beauty and honor in the soul. It is to prepare, not defenders of the nation, but a plague and a scourge for the human race" (*Militantis ecclesiae,* no.17). Pius XI considered the savage bloodshed of the First World War as a fruit of the secularized education in Europe (*UA*, nos.30-31).

By respecting the due governance of parents, civil authorities insure that their authority too will be respected. For children who learn obedience in the household will practice that obedience in the community and country. When the government fails to respect the just rule of parents over their children, they sow the seeds for rebellion. If children do not learn how to respect authority when they are young, how will they respect it as adults?

Benedict XV became pope in 1914, at the opening of the First World War. His first encyclical *Ad beatissimi apostolorum,* boldly declared that the cause of the war was the rejection of God's law in social and political affairs. Without any higher purpose, he explained, people cared only for wealth and power, and had nothing to restrain them from using force to obtain them. His efforts to assist in bringing peace to the warring nations of Europe was unsuccessful, but after the war he continued to preach a message of peace made possible by loving one another in Christ. He died of pneumonia in 1922.

Questions for Review

1) Why is it naturally just that parents have authority over their children, according to St. Thomas Aquinas?

2) What was the position of the Socialists and the Communists with regard to the government's respect for parental authority?

3) Why is it wrong for the state to force religious families to pay for non-religious schools?

4) Why have the Popes criticized secular schools?

5) How do religious schools act for the common good of society?

Lesson Seven:
Authority and Obedience

The fourth commandment also demands that we respect not only the authority of our parents, but also of those who hold authority within the larger communities of our cities and states (*CCC*, no.2234). Just as God's law demands that we obey our parents, so also we are bound to obey the lawfully appointed heads of the government, whether local, state or national.

It is a common error nowadays to think that all those who hold office in government receive their authority from the people. It is true that many of them were chosen for their office through elections. But that election does not create the power of the office. By nature, every community needs someone to oversee its activity and direct it to the common good. That is why every club or association will have a president, vice-president, and so on, to direct the activity of the group. The purpose of government is to help citizens achieve the common good within their community.

Authority is something established by God for our own good. Hence, all authority comes from God, who created our nature (*CCC*, no.2238). The Old Testament declares, "By me kings reign, and lawgivers decree just things. By me princes rule..." (*Prov.* 8:15-16). And elsewhere, "Over every nation he set a ruler" (*Ecclus.*17:14[*Sir.-NAB*]). All authority comes from God.

In the New Testament, we see the same teaching repeated. When Our Lord is brought before Pontius Pilate, Pilate asks Him, "Knowest thou not that I have power to crucify thee, and I have power to release thee?" Jesus does not respond by denying that Pilate has the power. Rather, He tells Pilate, "Thou shouldst not have any power against me, unless it were given thee from above" (*John* 19:10-11). In this passage, Jesus is showing us that all power, even in secular rulers such as Pontius Pilate, comes from Almighty God.

Both St. Peter and St. Paul echo this teaching. St. Peter in his *First Letter* writes "Be ye subject therefore to every human creature for God's sake: whether it be to the king as excelling; Or to governors as sent by him for the punishment of evildoers and for the praise of the good" (*1 Pet.* 2:13-14). St. Paul also directs Titus to tell his flock "...to be subject to princes and powers, to obey at a word..." (*Titus* 3:1).

In his *Letter to the Romans,* St. Paul goes so far as to say that if we disobey a legitimate authority, we sin gravely, and risk damnation.

> Let every soul be subject to higher powers. For there is no power but from God: and those that are ordained of God. Therefore, he that resisteth the power, resisteth the ordinance of God. And they that resist, purchase to themselves damnation (*Rom.* 13:1-2).

In modern times, we have fallen into the error of thinking that governments derive their powers from the consent of the governed. In this way, the citizens are, as it were, obeying themselves. This is the error of *Liberalism*. The Popes have pointed out that Liberalism destroys the virtue of obedience, which demands that we submit to others, not just ourselves. True authority demands true obedience. And there is no true authority that does not derive its power from God Himself. Leo XIII tells us:

> Those by whose authority the State is administered must be able so to compel the citizens to obedience that it is clearly a sin in the latter not to obey. But no man has in himself or of himself the power of constraining the free will of others by fetters of authority of this kind. This power resides solely in God, the Creator and Legislator of all things; and it is necessary that those who exercise it should do it as having received it from God (*Diuturnum illud,* no.11).

When a government makes laws against murder and theft, those laws are not something that man "invents." The government is following the laws that God has written in our hearts when He created our nature. How we punish murder and theft may vary from place to place, and from age to age, but *that* murder and theft are wrong is a part of every nation's law. This shows how all just human laws find their origin in the law of God.

Since all rulers who govern for the common good are following God's plan for ordering society, we are, of course, bound to obey them. The government is ruling in God's place. When the government rules unjustly, and makes laws against God's law, we are not bound to obey (*CCC*, no.2242). Indeed, it is a sin to obey a law that goes against the divine law. Hence, St. Peter told the Sanhedrin, "If it be just, in the sight of God, to hear you rather than God, judge ye" (*Acts* 4:19).

Bl. Pius IX reigned from 1846 to 1878. When he came to power, the Church was losing the last of her territories in Italy, and by the end of his reign, was limited to its present boundaries of the Vatican City. Pope Pius IX led the Church in a time when people were starting to make the nation and the secular state supreme over any religious authority. Even worse, many political groups, such as the Socialists and the Communists, were coming to power in revolutions and persecuting the Church. This happened not only in Europe, but also in Central and South America as well. Pope Pius addressed these errors in his encyclical letter *Quanta cura* and in the *Syllabus of Errors* (1864).

Questions for Review

1) Why is it false to believe that all authority comes from the choice of the people?

2) What does the Old Testament teach about the origin of authority? What does the New Testament teach?

3) How does the authority of God offer a foundation for all obedience?

4) How is it that all laws come from the law of God? Give an example.

Lesson Eight:

The Protection of Innocent Life

The next three commandments, namely *Thou shalt not kill, Thou shalt not commit adultery,* and *Thou shalt not steal,* protect the three most basic human goods, namely 1) life, 2) family and 3) material possessions (*CCC*, no.2198). Life is first, of course, because it is the good upon which all the other goods depend. Family is second, because one provides material goods for the sake of the family, not family for the sake of material goods. One need only remember how unhappy King Midas was when he touched his daughter, and she turned to gold! Even gold is worthless without the community of the family.

First, we will consider the fifth commandment, "Thou shalt not kill." *Thou shalt not kill* refers to men, and not to animals or plants. God told Noah "...Every thing that moveth and liveth shall be meat for you: even as the green herbs have I delivered them all to you" (*Gen.* 9:3).

While some have fallen into the erroneous belief that plants and animals are somehow "equal" with human beings, as Catholics we follow the word of Scripture, that plants and animals have been provided for us by God for our needs (*CCC*, no.2417). We must care for these creatures and always use them with good judgment and moderation, for God has made us stewards over His creation: "Increase and multiply, and fill the earth, and subdue it, and rule over the fishes of the sea, and the fowls of the air, and all living creatures that move upon the earth" (*Gen.* 1:28).

Men may use plants and animals for their needs, but they must never treat their fellow men in this way. The moral law demands that we act to preserve and protect human life. The gravity of sinning against the Fifth Commandment is shown in the story of Cain and Abel:

> And Cain said to Abel his brother: Let us go forth abroad. And when they were in the field, Cain rose up against his brother Abel, and slew him. And the Lord said to Cain: Where is thy brother Abel? And he answered, I know not: am I my brother's keeper? And He said to him: What hast thou done? The voice of thy brother's blood crieth to me from the earth (*Gen.* 4:8-10).

Pope John Paul II, commenting on this text remarks that "from this text the Church has taken the name of the 'sins which cry to God for justice,' and, first among them, she has included willful murder" (*Evangelium vitae*, no.9). The moral law decrees that the murder of the innocent is the gravest wrong that one can commit against one's neighbor. Hence, the laws of states and nations have as their first duty the protection of innocent life, and the punishment of those who violate the Fifth Commandment (*CCC*, no.2273).

A government that fails to protect the innocent undermines its own authority. While this may seem self-evident, many governments today no longer protect innocent life, but allow, even encourage the destruction of the innocent in their weakest and most vulnerable stages. **Abortion** kills innocent persons in their embryonic and fetal stages, while **infanticide** kills innocent persons soon after they are born. **Euthanasia** is the killing of innocent persons who are greatly weakened by sickness, old age or special needs, and it is sometimes called **"mercy killing,"** although there is nothing merciful about it.

This duty of the government to protect the lives of the innocent is so fundamental that the Popes have used the strongest language possible to remind statesmen of their responsibilities.

> Those who hold the reins of government should not forget that it is the duty of public authority by appropriate laws and sanctions to defend the lives of the innocent, and this all the more so since those whose lives are endangered and assailed cannot defend themselves. Among whom we must mention in the first place infants hidden in the mother's womb. And if the public magistrates not only do not defend them, but by their laws and ordinances betray them to death at the hands of doctors or of others, let them remember that God is the Judge and Avenger of innocent blood which cries from earth to Heaven (Pius XI, *Casti connubii,* no.67).

Political leaders are not excused from defending innocent life because of the "will of the majority" or "the voice of public opinion." No statesman may follow the majority where the majority works for injustice. We would not for a moment believe that a law was just that called for the execution or imprisonment of racial minorities. That would be contributing to a tyranny. As John Paul II tells us, "When a parliamentary or social majority decrees that it is legal, at least under certain conditions, to kill unborn human life, is it not really making a tyrannical decision with regard to the weakest and most defenseless of human beings?" (*Evangelium vitae,* no.70).

While some try to defend the murder of the innocent as a political necessity, others try to justify killing the innocent for medical or scientific benefits. Already the tissues of embryonic human persons and organs from aborted fetal humans are used for research. Related to this is the question of **human cloning**, or genetically produced human beings who are created solely for the purpose of "harvesting" their organs. The defenders of these gruesome experiments justify their work as "medically" necessary; on this view, the few must suffer for the common good.

Pope Pius XII addressed this question back in the 1950s. During the Second World War, both the Germans and the Japanese had performed experiments on the people they imprisoned. These were experiments that often led to the death of the subject. Pius XII pointed out that one could not apply the "common good" to justify these kinds of experiments: "in his personal being, man is not finally ordered to usefulness to society. On the contrary, the community exists for man" ("Moral Limits of Medical Research," no.28). The common good demands respect for *all* people, not some at the expense of others.

We cannot therefore allow human persons in their earliest stages of development to be used as a means for the cure of other people (*CCC*, no.2295). Pope John Paul II clearly teaches that "the use of human embryos or fetuses as an object of experimentation constitutes a crime against their dignity as human beings who have a right to the same respect owed to a child once born, just as to every person" (*Evangelium vitae*, no.63). One cannot respect human life, and sacrifice human infants for the cure of older people. Human embryos may be the smallest and least developed of human persons, but they are still persons. Hence, "The killing of innocent human creatures, even if carried out to help others, constitutes an absolutely unacceptable act" (*ibid*).

We must explore the common good further in regard to the questions of capital punishment and war. Public authority, based on the wrongdoing of the offending party, carries out both of these.

John Paul II became Pope in 1978 after the sudden death of Pope John Paul I, who reigned for only 33 days. He continued Pope Paul VI's task of implementing the reforms of the Second Vatican Ecumenical Council, especially in areas where a false or distorted interpretation of the Council had arisen. He reaffirmed the teaching of Pope Paul VI's *Populorum progressio* in his encyclical *Solicitudo rei socialis,* and updated the teaching of Pope Leo XIII's *Rerum novarum* in *Centesimus annus.* Perhaps Pope John Paul II's most outstanding contributions to Catholic social teaching are his defense of the natural law in *Veritatis splendor,* and his defense of the dignity of human life in *Evangelium vitae.*

Questions for Review

1) Why are the fifth, sixth and seventh commandments given in that order?

2) Why are men allowed to take the life of plants and animals?

3) How is the murder of the innocent a "sin that cries to heaven for vengeance"?

4) Why are countries not allowed to pass laws in favor of murder?

5) Why is it not permissible to perform harmful experiments on some group for the benefit of the common good?

6) Why is it wrong to destroy human embryos for the sake of medical advances?

Lesson Nine:
Capital Punishment

We saw earlier that when God commanded *Thou shalt not kill,* this did not apply to plants and animals. The commandment must be understood with other texts in Scripture. Similarly, while we read *Thou shalt not kill,* God later commands in the same book "Wizards thou shalt not suffer to live" (*Ex.* 22:18 [v.17-*NAB*]). And in the *Psalms,* David proclaims "In the morning I put to death all the wicked of the land" (*Ps.*100:8 [101-*NAB*]). In general, the Old Law inflicted the death penalty for grievous crimes, that is, those committed against God, and for murder, kidnapping, irreverence towards one's parents, adultery and incest. How are we then to understand this in light of the commandment *Thou shalt not kill?*

When God forbids killing, He is speaking primarily of *innocent* people. Nothing can ever justify the killing of the innocent. There are, however, circumstances in which the public authority justly takes the life of the guilty. St. Thomas explains those circumstances in the following way:

Every part is naturally for the sake of the whole. For this reason we observe that if the health of the whole body demands the cutting away of a member, through its being decayed or infectious to the other members, it will be both praiseworthy and advantageous to have it cut away. Now every one is compared to the whole community, as part to whole. Therefore if a man be dangerous and infectious to the community, on account of some sin, it is praiseworthy and advantageous that he be killed in order to safeguard the common good, since "a little leaven corrupts the whole lump" (*1 Cor.* 5:6) (IIaIIae,Q.64,art.2).

The public authority has as its first duty the protection of the innocent (*CCC*, no.2265). When it takes the life of the guilty, it does this in fulfillment of its duty. When a government imposes the death penalty after a fair trail, it does not do so from vengeance or hatred. Quite the contrary — the government should always apply punishment out of love — primarily love for the common good (cf. *Summa*, Ia,Q19, art.6; IaIIae, Q.19, art.10).

Some might object that the "right to life" is absolute, and can never be taken away. Pius XII answered this objection long ago when he declared:

> Even when there is question of the execution of a condemned man, the state does not dispose of the individual's right to life. In this case it is reserved to the public power to deprive the condemned person of the enjoyment of life in expiation of his crime when, by his crime, he has already disposed himself of his right to live ("Moral Limits of Medical Research," no.33).

The circumstances requiring capital punishment have changed. We are now better able to protect the innocent without recourse to the death penalty. As John Paul II teaches, we "ought not go to the extreme of executing the offender except in cases of absolute necessity: in other words, when it would not be possible otherwise to defend society. Today however, as a result of steady improvements in the organization of the penal system, such cases are very rare, if not practically non-existent" (*Evangelium vitae,* no.56).

When Pope John Paul speaks of "improvements in the organization of the penal system," he means that we are now better able to arrest, convict and secure those who are dangerous to society. Up until recent times, no society could afford to house large numbers of criminals in a safe or healthy way for long periods of time. Society had no other way of protecting itself against dangerous criminals other than the death penalty. When society is able to protect itself without use of the death penalty, it should do so.

Hence the *Catechism of the Catholic Church* teaches:

> If, however, non-lethal means are sufficient to defend and protect people's safety from the aggressor, authority will limit itself to such means, as these are more in keeping with the concrete conditions of the common good and more in conformity with the dignity of the human person (*CCC,* no.2267).

Sadly, it may well be that in some time in the future, we could become unable to protect society through our prisons, and once more, we may have to turn to the death penalty. What must always come first, in any consideration of the death penalty, is the common good and the protection of the innocent.

St. Thomas Aquinas was born in 1225, the son of a noble family, and joined the newly founded Order of Preachers (Dominicans) at the age of 18. Honored as the Common Doctor of the Church, St. Thomas wrote many works of theology, which continue to be studied to the present day. His best known work is the *Summa Theologiae,* a comprehensive textbook that covers the range of topics in theology: God, the angels, creation, the human soul, the virtues, the Incarnation, the sacraments, etc. In his treatment of the different kinds of law (eternal, natural, human, divine), St. Thomas provides the most basic principles for Catholic social teaching. Many of the early social encyclicals by popes such as Leo XIII draw heavily from St. Thomas. Indeed, both Pope Leo XIII and Pope Pius XI devoted whole encyclicals to the importance of the theology of St. Thomas Aquinas.

Questions for Review

1) How do we know that "you shall not kill" does not forbid capital punishment?

2) How does St. Thomas show the necessity for capital punishment?

3) How does Pius XII answer the objection that capital punishment violates the criminal's "right to life"?

4) Why does Pope John Paul II believe that capital punishment should be abolished? Is this a "change" in the teaching of the Church?

Lesson Ten:

Is It Always Sinful to Wage War?

The fifth commandment declares *Thou shalt not kill.* Does this mean that the killing that soldiers do in war is always wrong? Again, we must look at what God Himself commands in the Scriptures after He has given the commandment, *Thou shalt not kill.*

After the Hebrew people entered the Promised Land, God orders them to wage war on the people who live there. "And the Lord said to Joshua: Fear not, nor be thou dismayed: take with thee all the multitude of fighting men, arise and go up to the town of Hai: Behold I have delivered into thy hand the king thereof, and the people, and the city, and the land" (*Jos.* 8:1). When God commanded the Israelites not to kill, this forbade from taking life as private persons. As soldiers under a lawful authority however, they are not taking life for their private good, but in defense of the common good.

To take another example, the high priest Samuel commanded Saul on God's behalf to attack the city of Amalec: "Thus saith the Lord of hosts: I have reckoned up all that Amalec hath done to Israel: how he opposed them in the way when they came up out of Egypt. Now therefore go, and smite Amalec, and utterly destroy all that he hath: spare him not, nor covet any thing that is his: but slay both man and woman, child and suckling, ox and sheep, camel and ass" (*1Kings* 15:2-3 [*1 Sam.-NAB*]).

Some people will grant that God in the Old Testament allows and even commands war, but they think that this permission changes in the New Testament. In their view, Jesus would never allow warfare. Against this opinion, St. Augustine, however, makes the following argument:

> If the Christian Religion forbade war altogether, those who sought salutary advice in the Gospel would rather have been counseled to cast aside their arms, and to give up soldiering altogether. On the contrary, they were told: "Do violence to no man, neither accuse any falsely, and be content with your wages," the command to be content with their wages manifestly implying no prohibition to continue in the service" (*Letter to Marcellinus* 138, chap.2, n.15).

It is true that Jesus tells us in the Sermon on the Mount: "Blessed are the peacemakers." But, as St. Thomas Aquinas points out, "Those who wage war justly aim at peace, and so they are not opposed to peace, except to the evil peace, which Our Lord 'came not to send upon earth'" (*Matt.* 10:34). Hence Augustine says: "For peace is not sought in order to the kindling of war, but war is waged in order that peace may be obtained. Therefore, even in waging war, cherish the spirit of a peacemaker, that, by conquering those whom you attack, you may lead them back to the advantages of peace" (*Letter to Boniface*, 189, n.6).

In the course of his writings, St. Augustine gave three conditions for a war to be just. These three conditions were repeated in the teachings of St. Thomas, and have become a part of Catholic moral teaching.

1. First, the war must be declared by a due authority. The due authority is the justly empowered government that has the care for the common good. Private individuals cannot "declare war" on behalf of their country. War must be declared by the lawful authority. In the words of St. Augustine, "the natural order which seeks the peace of mankind, ordains that the monarch should have the power of undertaking war if he thinks it advisable" (*Against Faustus*, Bk.22, §75).

2. Second, the war must be waged for a just cause. The clearest case of a just cause is self-defense against invasion. In *Gaudium et spes* (*The Pastoral Constitution on the Church in the Modern World*), we read that "as long as the danger of war persists and there is no international authority with the necessary competence and power, governments cannot be denied the right of lawful self-defense, once all peace efforts have failed" (*GS* no.79, §4). St. Augustine for his part gives other examples of causes that are just: "A just war is wont to be described as one that avenges wrongs, when a nation or state has to be punished, for refusing to make amends for the wrongs inflicted by its subjects, or to restore what it has seized unjustly" (*QQ. in Hept.,* qu. 10, *super Jos.*, cited by St. Thomas, *Summa, IaIIae,* Q.40, art.1).

3. Finally, the lawful authorities must carry out the war with a right intention. As St. Thomas explains, "For it may happen that the war is declared by the legitimate authority, and for a just cause, and yet be rendered unlawful through a wicked intention. Hence Augustine says (*Against Faustus,* Bk.22, §74): 'The passion for inflicting harm, the cruel thirst for vengeance, an unpacific and relentless spirit, the fever of revolt, the lust of power, and such like things, all these are rightly condemned in war.'"

When a war lacks any of these conditions, it is not truly a just war. Following the spiritual direction of their priests or the directives of their bishops, Catholics may object in conscience to participating in an unjust war. The Church asks nations to respect the right of those religious sects who object in conscience to war of any kind, but Catholic teaching does not allow for a conscientious objection to all war as such. As Pius XII explains:

> If, therefore, a body representative of the people and a government — both having been chosen by free elections — in a moment of extreme danger decides, by legitimate instruments of internal and external policy, on defensive precautions, and carries out plans which they consider necessary, it does not act immorally. Therefore a Catholic citizen cannot invoke his own conscience in order to refuse to serve and fulfill those duties the law imposes (Christmas Address of 1956, in *Major Addresses of Pius XII*, p. 225).

This teaching is reaffirmed in the *Catechism of the Catholic Church*. While the *Catechism* declares that "Public authorities should make equitable provision for those who for reasons of conscience refuse to bear arms..."(no.2311), nonetheless, it states "Public authorities, in this case, [i.e., of a just war] have the right and duty to impose on citizens *the obligations necessary for national defense*" (no.2311; cf. *GS* 79, § 3). (emphasis in original)

St. Augustine was born in 354 in the town of Hippo in northern Africa, and died in the final days of the Roman Empire in 430. He is generally recognized as the greatest authority among the Church Fathers, even by many Protestants. In his classic work *The City of God,* St. Augustine explains how Christians should never let this world become an end in itself, but always work for the glory of God and His saints in the "City of God." His discussion of just war, the religious obligations of society, and the nature and primacy of the common good influenced Catholic thinking for centuries.

Questions for Review

1) Does the commandment "you shall not kill" outlaw every kind of warfare?

2) Why does St. Augustine believe that Jesus did not outlaw warfare?

3) What are the three conditions for a just war?

4) Who is a "due authority"? What makes a cause "just"?

5) What does St. Thomas Aquinas mean by a "right intention"?

6) Under what circumstances may a Catholic "conscientiously object" to participating in a war?

Lesson Eleven:
Marriage and Divorce

After the precept *Thou shalt not kill* comes the precept *Thou shalt not commit adultery* (*Ex.* 20:14). While the fifth commandment protects the good of life, the sixth commandment protects the good of the family (*CCC*, nos.2380-2381). Because of this, some may fall into the error of thinking that the sixth commandment does not pertain to the social teaching of the Church. Social teaching concerns the society at large, and hence the family belongs to some other consideration.

But this is wrong. The social teaching of the Church addresses all matters that pertain to the common good. And the future of any society depends on the stability of its marriages and the upbringing of its children (*CCC*, nos.2207-2211). Hence, Catholic social teaching addresses marriage and family insofar as they contribute to the common good of society.

To understand this, we must first see why God instituted marriage. The offspring of the beasts do not require both parents for their upbringing. A mother is sufficient for the care of dogs or cows. Dogs and cows do not need their male parent to grow up well. For us, the case is quite different. As St. Thomas Aquinas explains:

It is evident that the upbringing of a human child requires not only the mother's care for his nourishment, but also much more the care of his father as guide and guardian, and under whom he progresses in goods both internal and external. Hence human nature rebels against an undetermined union of the sexes and demands that a man should be united to a determinate woman and should stay with her a long time or even for a whole lifetime. Hence it is that in the human race the male has a natural care for the certainty of offspring, because on him falls the upbringing of the child: and this certainly would cease if the union of sexes were undetermined (*IIaIIae,* Q.154, a.2).

Note that St. Thomas claims that a father does not merely provide food or money, but that he is a "guide and guardian." He should give an example to his sons of how to be a good man, and an example to his daughters of what to seek in a good husband.

By nature then, the union of man and woman should be permanent for the good of the children. The children are a kind of "common good" of the man and woman, for they are not completely of the mother, nor completely of the father, but rather stand as a good shared by both (cf. Pope John Paul II, *Letter to Families,* no.11).

All societies on earth have some form of marriage, some way of binding in a lasting way men to women for the sake of their children. In the beginning, God joined Adam to Eve, one man to one woman. Over time, as fallen man became more and more confused about the moral law, societies legalized all sorts of customs contrary to the good of marriage. Some societies allowed men to take several wives. Other societies allowed sexual relations outside of marriage. Even among the Hebrews who were guided by the divine law, Moses allowed divorce because of the "hardness" of their hearts (*Matt.* 19:8). All of these went against the nature that God had given to man. As Our Lord declared to the Jews, who asked Him about divorce:

> ...Answering, [He] said to them: Have ye not read, that he who made man from the beginning, made them male and female? And he said: For this cause shall a man leave father and mother, and shall cleave to his wife, and they two shall be in one flesh. Therefore now they are not two, but one flesh. What therefore God hath joined together, let no man put asunder (*Matt.* 19:4-6).

With the coming of Our Lord and the establishment of His Church, marriage was restored to its former dignity. Indeed, marriage was elevated to a sacrament, a means whereby God gives grace to the husband and wife. The sacramental status of marriage excludes any possibility of divorce, for what "God hath joined together, let no man put asunder" (*Matt.* 19:6).

Divorce would attempt to find a human way around a divine institution. But Our Lord makes clear that no one can seek a divorce without violating the sixth commandment: "Everyone that putteth away his wife and marries another, committeth adultery and he that marries her that is put away from her husband committeth adultery" (*Luke* 16:18). Divorce is a form of oath breaking, for the couple swore at the altar to take each other in marriage until parted by death (*CCC*, no.2384).

It should then come as no surprise that the Catholic Church has always steadfastly defended the permanent bond of matrimony, and resisted even the wealthy and powerful when they have sought to bend her laws for their own worldly gain. Leo XIII relates that "all generations of men will admire the proofs of unbending courage which are to be found in the decrees of Nicholas I against Lothair; of Urban II and Paschal II against Philip I of France; of Celestine III and Innocent III against Alphonsus of Leon and Philip II of France; of Clement VII and Paul III against Henry VIII; and, lastly, of Pius VII, that holy and courageous pontiff, against Napoleon I, when at the height of his prosperity and in the fullness of his power" (*Arcanum,* no.34).

Perhaps it is unclear to us who live in an age when divorce is so common why the Church would defend marriage so vigorously. Not only does the Church recognize the threat to souls through violation of the sixth commandment, but also the threat to the temporal good of nations and peoples (*CCC,* no.2385). The warnings of Pope Leo XIII in 1880 sound like a catalogue of our present day social problems:

> Truly, it is hardly possible to describe how great are the evils that flow from divorce. Matrimonial contracts are by it made variable; mutual kindness is weakened; deplorable inducements to unfaithfulness are supplied; harm is done to the education and training of children; occasion is afforded for the breaking up of homes; the seeds of dissension are sown among families; the dignity of womanhood is lessened and brought low, and women run the risk of being deserted after having ministered to the pleasures of men. Since, then, nothing has such power to lay waste families and destroy the mainstay of kingdoms as the corruption of

74

morals, it is easily seen that divorces are in the highest degree hostile to the prosperity of families and States, springing as they do from the depraved morals of the people, and, as experience shows us, opening out a way to every kind of evil-doing in public and in private life (*Arcanum*, no. 29).

When people promote the lawfulness of divorce, they often focus on particular cases of people who have married badly. Why should couples be forced to stay married if they are unhappy? Why should a woman stay married to a man who is routinely drunk or abusive? Why should a man stay married to a woman who no longer loves him, or has left him for another man? Cases such as these lead us to think that divorce should be allowed under some circumstances.

These hard cases do not change the fact that God instituted marriage, and that no one on earth has the power to break apart what He has joined. But even if the Church did have the power to grant divorces, as the Protestant communities believe they do, the institution of marriage would be gravely undermined. Indeed, the practice of divorce within the Protestant communities has revealed this. As Leo XIII explains,

At the beginning, Protestants allowed legalized divorces in certain although but few cases, and yet from the affinity of circumstances of like kind, the number of divorces increased to such extent in Germany, America, and elsewhere that all wise thinkers deplored the boundless corruption of morals, and judged the recklessness of the laws to be simply intolerable (*ibid*).

One can illustrate this point with examples from our own country. When Leo XIII wrote *Arcanum* in 1880, only 4 out of 100 marriages ended in divorce in the United States (National Center for Health Statistics). By the time Pius XI had written *Casti connubii* in 1929, 17 out of 100 marriages ended in divorce. The divorce rate had grown three times as great! When Pope Paul VI wrote *Humanae Vitae* in 1968, 33 out of 100 marriages ended in divorce. By the time Pope John Paul II wrote *Familiaris consortio* in 1981, roughly 50 out of 100 marriages ended in divorce. (Bear in mind these numbers represent total marriages, which would then include people who are marrying more than once). It is easy to understand why the Second Vatican Council condemned divorce as a "plague" (*Gaudium et spes*, no.47§2; *CCC*, no.2385). Plainly, the legalization of divorce has undermined the ability of people to stay married at all.

Why is this? Because of our fallen human nature, married couples need God's grace in their lives. One cannot allow divorce without denying matrimony's sacramental status. That is why the Protestant communities allow divorce; they deny that Christ instituted marriage as a sacrament, against the word of St. Paul: "This is a great sacrament" (*Eph.* 5:32). Without God's grace, however, working in the marriage, our passions prevent the husband and wife from offering themselves to each other in self-sacrificial love. As Pope Leo XIII observed in his own time "divorce once being tolerated, there will be no restraint powerful enough to keep it within the bounds marked out or presurmised. Great indeed is the force of example, and even greater still the might of passion" (*Arcanum,* no.30).

Let no one then make the mistake of underestimating the importance of Catholic social teaching on the indissolubility of marriage. Once the teaching of the Church is rejected on this essential matter, we have little or no way of keeping families intact. Our contemporary acceptance of divorce, in the grave words of Pope Leo XIII "tends to the certain destruction of society" (*Arcanum,* no.32).

Pius XI reigned from 1922 to 1939, over the period of time which in the United States was called the "Jazz Age," followed by the Great Depression. He took as his papal motto "The Peace of Christ in the Kingdom of Christ." His encyclical letters on marriage (*Casti connubii*) and education (*Divini Illius Magistri*) remain to this day as the most recent encyclicals on these topics. *Casti connubii* defended Church teaching against those who wished to poison family life with legal divorce, abortion, sterilization and contraception, while *Divini Illius Magistri* defended the Catholic understanding of education in which religion was an essential part. Pope Pius XI updated the teaching of Pope Leo XIII's encyclical *Rerum novarum* in *Quadragesimo anno,* which repeated Pope Leo's criticisms of economic liberalism and socialism. He condemned the various forms of political oppression that threatened the world at that time: atheistic communism in *Divini Redemptoris,* National Socialism (Nazism) of Germany in *Mit Brennender Sorge,* and Italian Fascism in *Non abbiamo bisogno.* Fundamental to his whole pontificate was the proclamation of the social reign of Jesus Christ, which he emphasized by instituting the Feast of Christ the King (*Quas primas*).

Questions for Review

1) How does the sixth commandment pertain to society?

2) Why do human beings need to join in permanent unions for their offspring?

3) Why is divorce contrary to God's law?

4) How does history show the seriousness of the Church in defense of the marriage bond?

5) What are the social problems that divorce allows?

6) Why cannot one allow divorce for "exceptional" cases?

7) Why is it important to remember that marriage is a sacrament?

Lesson Twelve:
Contraception and the Common Good

Nothing might seem a more personal matter than how many children a couple chooses to bring into the world. And yet, the choice to welcome or limit children has enormous social consequences. Because of the influence of "population scares," we usually think that a society is doomed when there are "too many" children. Pope John Paul II notes "a certain panic deriving from the studies of ecologists and futurologists on population growth, which sometimes exaggerate the danger of demographic increase to the quality of life," a situation from which "an anti-life mentality is born" (*Familiaris consortio*, no.30).

But the truth is exactly the reverse. A society is doomed when families do not have enough children to replace the generation that passes away. Simply put, a society without children is a society without a future.

While some nations struggle to develop their resources in a way that will provide for a growing population, other nations, in particular the wealthiest and most developed, are suffering from an enormous decline in the birthrate. John Paul II has called attention to this problem in his 1987 encyclical *Sollicitudo rei socialis*. He writes:

One cannot deny the existence, especially in the southern hemisphere, of a demographic problem which creates difficulties for development. One must immediately add that in the northern hemisphere the nature of this problem is reversed: here, the cause for concern is the drop in the birthrate, with repercussions on the aging of the population, unable even to renew itself biologically. In itself, this is a phenomenon capable of hindering development (no.25).

In order for a country to achieve "replacement levels" of population, each woman must have an average of 2.3 children. Once the average number dips below this, the population over the long run will start to decline. With the exception of Ireland, Israel and New Zealand, none of the "First World" nations are close to replacement levels. The average number of children per woman in the United States is 1.8, in Switzerland and Austria 1.4 and in Spain 1.13 (UN Department of Economic and Social Affairs-Population Division). All the Holy Father has to do is look out his window to see that there is a problem – the average Italian woman has 1.4 children. Pope John Paul II describes this as "a disturbing decline or collapse of the birthrate" (*Evangelium vitae*, no.16).

Here is an easy way to think about underpopulation. If every man and woman had two children, they would replace themselves. That would keep the population constant. But of course, not everyone is able or willing to have children. Further, some children will not live to maturity. Hence, those who have children must have more than two, just to keep the population constant.

Three children would be enough if *everyone* married and had children. But of course, some segment of the population will never marry or have children. Another segment of the population will be infertile for physical reasons. Hence, those who have children must make up for those who do not. That means that every couple must have *more than three*, just to keep the population constant. A society that discourages big families (unless it welcomes immigrants) begins to shrink over time.

What does John Paul II mean when he says that this shrinking of the population can "hinder development"? A smaller number of young people means a smaller number of workers to support a growing population of prospective retirees. This means a smaller number of taxpayers supporting programs for retired senior citizens. In 1985, there were five workers for every one retiree. By 2010, the number will be four to one, and by 2035, that number will shrink to two to one (Social Security Administration data).

A smaller number of children also means a smaller number of students for our schools and colleges. Spain over the last eight years lost 326,330 students in Catholic schools, and 1.25 million in public schools. In this country, colleges and universities that expanded during the post-World War II period will shrink considerably from want of students (*Zenit*, Jan.17, 2001).

At the same time, the wealthy nations of the world impose birth control on poorer nations as a means of controlling their future strength. To continue that passage cited above from *Sollicitudo rei socialis*, John Paul II writes:

[I]t is very alarming to see governments in many countries launching systematic campaigns against birth, contrary not only to the cultural and religious identity of the countries themselves but also contrary to the nature of true development. It often happens that these campaigns are the result of pressure and financing coming from abroad, and in some cases they are made a condition for the granting of financial and economic aid and assistance. In any event, there is an absolute lack of respect for the freedom of choice of the parties involved, men and women often subjected to intolerable pressures, including economic ones, in order to force them to submit to this new form of oppression. It is the poorest populations which suffer such mistreatment, and this sometimes leads to a tendency towards a form of racism, or the promotion of certain equally racist forms of eugenics (no.25).

Oftentimes, the wealthier nations will provide economic aid to poorer nations only on the condition that they accept "family planning programs" which include artificial birth control, sterilization and abortion. It is however not truly compassionate to assist some people in a country by killing others, or contracepting them out of existence (*CCC*, no.2372). Pope John Paul II describes this practice in the harshest possible terms: "These policies are extending their field of action by the use of new techniques, to the point of poisoning the lives of millions of defenseless human beings, as if in a form of 'chemical warfare'" (*Centesimus annus*, no.39).

One must also consider the social problems that arise from population control. A country that accepts such programs will soon have the same imbalances in its population as the wealthy countries — a great number of older people and a small number of younger people to care for them. Further, some countries have developed terrible imbalances between male and female children. When families are limited to one or two children, many societies will often choose to have boys instead of girls. Over time, the number of males exceeds the number of females, leaving many young men without the possibility of marriage and family.

This is a hard saying for us because we think of the number of children that we have as entirely a personal matter. We may think that a large family is undesirable because it often prevents one from enjoying an abundance of material possessions or opportunities for leisure. Certainly, there are quite legitimate prudential reasons for spacing out births by natural means (e.g. natural family planning), which arise from the physical or psychological needs of the husband and wife, or from other grave circumstances (cf. *Humanae vitae*, no.16).

But we cannot as a matter of course limit our families in order to enjoy those things which previous ages would have immediately recognized as luxuries. This would make wealth and amusement the end of family life. As John Paul II tells us, we are not allowed to "consider children as one of the many 'things' which an individual can have or not have, according to taste, and which compete with other possibilities" (*Centesimus annus*, no.39).

Rather, the end of the family is the moral and spiritual growth of all the members of the family, especially the children. The more children one has, the greater the opportunity for growth in selfless love and generosity. As we read in *Gaudium et spes*

(*The Pastoral Constitution on the Church in the Modern World*), "Among the couples who fulfill their God-given task in this way, those merit special mention who with wise and shared deliberation, courageously undertake the proper upbringing of even a larger number of children" (50§2; *CCC*, no.2373).

Since the family is the most basic division of the society, the number of children that a family has, or does not have, has enormous social consequences. At bottom, many of us in the prosperous nations have rejected God's commandment to "be fruitful and multiply." God created us from nothing, and gave us the gift of sharing in His creative power through procreation. One might see a fittingness in our crisis of "underpopulation," in that we are suffering the consequences of rejecting God's commandment by returning to the nothingness from which He created us. Indeed, "the wages of sin is death" (*Rom.* 6:23) — not only for individuals, but also for societies.

Paul VI reigned from 1963 to 1978. He ascended the throne in the second year of the Second Vatican Ecumenical Council, and devoted his papacy to implementing its teachings. Paul VI warned against the morally and socially destructive effects of artificial birth control in *Humanae vitae*, accurately predicting that governments would use unjust methods to reduce population. In *Populorum progressio*, he reminded men that societies needed to grow not only in wealth and technology,

but also in moral virtue and spiritual devotion. He criticized the early forms of communist influence on the faith, later known as "liberation theology" (*Evangelii nuntiandi*).

Questions for Review

1) What does it mean for a country to have "a collapse in the birthrate"? How many children must the average couple have to replace themselves? Why are large families necessary for population stability?

2) What could Pope John Paul II mean when he says that a drop in the birthrate is harmful to the development of a society?

3) In what way are the wealthier nations imposing their problems on poorer nations?

4) What problems do many nations have as a result of severely limiting the number of children they have?

5) What are good reasons for limiting the number of children one has? What are bad reasons? How do people misunderstand the purpose of the family?

6) What is the advantage of a big family for the family itself? What are the advantages of big families for the society as a whole?

Lesson Thirteen:
Man's Stewardship over Nature

The seventh commandment tells us *Thou shalt not steal* (*Ex.* 20:15; *Deut.* 5:19). This means that we may not take possessions that belong to our neighbor. If we would understand this commandment, we first must understand why human beings need to take exterior goods to themselves as their property.

We read in *Genesis* that God created man and gave him dominion over all of nature: "...Let him have dominion over the fishes of the sea, and the fowls of the air, and the beasts, and the whole earth, and every creeping creature that moveth upon the earth" (*Gen.* 1:26). We know this not only by revelation, but also by natural reason. Aristotle for example explains that in the natural order, the lower is for the sake of the higher. Plants for example serve as food for animals. Hence, plants and animals are both for the sake of man: "Wherefore it is not unlawful if man use plants for the good of animals, and animals for the good of man" (*Politics*, Bk. I, Chap. 8). Hence God commanded, "Behold I have given you every herb bearing seed upon the earth, and all trees that have in themselves seed of their own kind, to be your meat" (*Gen.* 1:29), and again, "And every thing that moveth and liveth shall be meat for you..." (*Gen.* 9:3).

Man's lordship over nature carries with it moral responsibilities. Our treatment of animals, plants and the whole of nature is therefore a stewardship for which we must give an account (*CCC*, no.2417). A steward does not own the house or property, but rather takes care of it for his master. We are stewards under God's governance. As John Paul II writes:

> Man's lordship however is not absolute, but ministerial: it is a real reflection of the unique and infinite lordship of God. Hence man must exercise it with wisdom and love, sharing in the boundless wisdom and love of God (*Evangelium vitae,* no.52).

Man's use of nature must then be limited by the moral law such that we use things in a way pleasing to God. While the Old Testament allowed men to kill animals for his survival, it also forbade actions that seemed like cruelty to them. Hence God forbids the Hebrews to kill a mother bird along with her brood *(Deut.* 22:6) and commands them "Thou shalt not muzzle the ox that treadeth out thy corn on the floor" *(Deut.* 25:4). For if men feel pity toward the suffering of animals, they are more likely to take pity on their fellow men: "The just regardeth the lives of his beasts: but the bowels of the wicked are cruel" *(Prov.* 12:10).

While animals should be treated without cruelty (*CCC,* no.2418), they do not have "rights" in the modern meaning of that word. Animals cannot make claims of justice on human beings. The attempt to make animals in some way equal to mankind is similar to the errors of the pagans, who revered certain animals and considered them unusable by man. The ancient Egyptians for example revered sheep and goats. While our use of animals is subject to the moral law, this elevation of animals to a dignity equal to our own is a crime against the natural order, for only man is made to the image and likeness of God:

"Let us make man to our image and likeness: and let him have dominion..." *(Gen.* 1:26).

While some view the needs of human beings and the well being of plants and animals as if they were equal parties, some go even further and see the very existence of mankind as a threat to nature. Such people work actively to limit human population, especially through artificial birth control and abortion. They fail to understand that these are crimes against nature, and that if people are callous toward their own offspring, they cannot be expected to treat the rest of creation as loving stewards.

Pope John Paul II has lamented that although people are worried "about preserving the natural habitats of the various animal species threatened with extinction...too little effort is made to safeguard the moral conditions for an authentic 'human ecology'," a human ecology which allows the family to be "the sanctuary of life" (*Centesimus annus,* nos.38-39). For the most natural form of stewardship entrusted to us is over our own offspring. As St. Thomas Aquinas explains, abortion is a crime against nature, "since even the beasts look forward to their offspring" (*Book IV Commentary on the Four Books of Sentences*, dist. 31 qu. 2 art. 3 Exposition).

The excessive concern for both plants and animals flows from the modern denial of Divine Providence. Because many people deny that the well-being of nature depends primarily on God, the conservation of nature seems to depend wholly on man. In fact, the continuous restoration of ecological harmony in spite of ice ages, volcanic eruptions and even the mass extinction of species reveals the power of nature under God's providence:

"Are not two sparrows sold for a farthing? and not one of them shall fall on the ground without your Father" *(Matt.* 10:29). Man is quite capable of damaging the parts of nature, but Scripture shows the ultimate governance and preservation of nature belongs to God: "What thou givest to them they shall gather up: when thou openest thy hand, they shall all be filled with good. But if thou turnest away thy face, they shall be troubled: thou shalt take away their breath, and they shall fail, and shall return to their dust" *(Ps.* 103:28-29[*Ps.*104-*NAB*).

The question is not then how man may "save" the planet, but how he may best take care of the natural things that fall under his care. State management is one way, but Catholic social teaching does not teach this as the only way or the best way. St. Thomas Aquinas taught long ago that private ownership best disposes men to develop prudence and charity in relation to natural things. Hence, Catholic social teaching has always defended private ownership as a means for preserving the common good. The stewardship that farmers exercise over their animals, for example, preserves them for the good of all.

As the population becomes more urbanized, and people live farther from the sources of their food, the place for man's share in God's providence, and indeed his sense of God's providence becomes greatly reduced. That is why in recent years the popes have given special attention to farming and rural life. Pius XII praised the farming community of Italy since they lived in "continual contact with nature," in places "remote from the excess of an artificial civilization" *(Speech to Farm Owners and Operators,* Nov. 15, 1946). Blessed Pope John XXIII praised the way that farmers "live in close harmony with nature," a life "rich in allusions to God the Creator and Provider" *(Mater et magistra,* no.144). It is important to remember that, according to the teaching of *Genesis,* agriculture is the first of the arts.

The Catholic teaching on stewardship, based on a tradition that goes back to the opening chapters of *Genesis,* offers a middle course between a pagan "worship" of nature at the expense of the common good, and a modern "management" of nature that substitutes man for God by exaggerating man's technical ability. Man must care for the plants and animals that God has given for his use, yet he must not care for them as if their survival depended on his limited efforts. On the contrary, the modern rejection of Divine Providence would deprive us of the ability to understand how to order ourselves rightly to God, to nature and finally, even to each other.

St. Isidore the Laborer, an 11th century Spanish saint, is considered the patron of farmers. His day of work began every morning with Mass, and there are several stories of angels assisting him in his work. His feast day on May 15, which he shares with his wife St. Maria, is frequently observed as a day dedicated to remembering the work of agricultural stewardship. It is one of several days in the liturgical calendar significant to farmers. The "Ember Days" were prescribed for the calendar for three days (Wednesday, Friday and Saturday) at the beginning of each of the four seasons, and included prayer and penance for the sake of offering thanksgiving

to God for the gifts of nature, and petition for an abundant harvest. The "Rogation Days" (the 25th of April, called the "Major" Rogation, and three days preceding Ascension Thursday, known as the "Minor") were also days of prayer and penance dedicated to asking for mercy from God's anger and protection from natural disaster, as well as a fruitful harvest for the coming year.

Questions for Review

1) How do we know that it is fair for human beings to use plants and animals as food and clothing? Do we know this only from the Bible?

2) Why are we not allowed to use plants and animals any way we please?

3) What commands did the Old Testament give about the care of animals? Does this mean that animals have rights?

4) Why do some people fall into the error of thinking they have to "save" the earth from destruction?

5) Why have the popes in modern times spoken on the importance of farm life?

Lesson Fourteen:
Private Ownership and Common Use

While by natural justice, the earth belongs to all men in common, the human law divides up the earth among particular men. As St. Thomas Aquinas explains, "the distinction of possessions...[was] not brought in by nature, but devised by human reason for the benefit of human life" (*IaIIae,* Q.94, a.5, 3rd reply). As he remarks elsewhere, "For if a particular piece of land be considered absolutely, it contains no reason why it should belong to one man more than to another" (*IIaIIae,* Q.57, a.3). Why does the human law divide up property among different men instead of treating it as common?

To answer this, we must contrast men to the beasts. Animals guided by instinct have no need of property. They are able to nourish themselves and reproduce using only temporary shelters and territory. Man on the other hand lives by reason. He must farm or hunt for his food, and build his shelters for his protection. While the animals can fulfill their needs in the short term, man needs to take things to himself for his long-term good.

Hence, man takes exterior goods to himself, e.g. land, animals and houses that he may live and perfect himself. While no piece of land belongs to one man rather than another by nature, nonetheless as St. Thomas explains, "if it be considered in respect of its adaptability to cultivation, and the unmolested use of the land, it has a certain fittingness to be the property of one and not of another man" (*IIaIIae,* Q.57, a.3).

While everyone understands that there must be some division of property among men, not everyone understands that some property must be "private," that is, the exclusive possession of a particular man. Some people make the mistake of thinking that if everything belongs to the "community," everyone will be happier. How can people envy each other, if no one owns more than anyone else? How can people become greedy, if they cannot own anything in the first place?

Catholic social teaching however has always defended private property. St. Augustine condemned a heretical group called the "Apostles," who "with extreme arrogance have given themselves that name because they do not admit into their communion persons who are married or possess anything of their own" (*De Haeres,* haer. 40, cited by St. Thomas, *Summa, IIaIIae,* Q.66, art.2). It is good for people to own their own things (*CCC*, no.2402).

St. Thomas Aquinas gives three reasons for this (*IIaIIae* Q.66, a.2):

1) First, because every man is more careful to procure what is for himself alone than that which is common to many or to all: since each one would shirk the labor and leave to another that which concerns the community.

2) Secondly, because human affairs are conducted in more orderly fashion if each man is charged with taking care of some particular thing himself, whereas there would be con-

fusion if everyone had to look after any one thing indeterminately.

3) Thirdly, because a more peaceful state is ensured to man if each one is contented with his own. Hence it is to be observed that quarrels arise more frequently where there is no division of the things possessed.

It is true that, if we allow people to have their own possessions, some will have more than others. But this is part of God's providence. As St. Thomas explains, "whatever certain people have in superabundance is due, by natural law, to the purpose of aiding the poor" (*IIaIIae* Q.66, a.7). God could give to the poor by daily miracles, but instead, He gives to some in abundance . so that they might assist His work by helping those in need (*CCC*, nos.2404-2405). As St. Thomas tells us, "each one is entrusted with the stewardship of his own things, so that out of them he may come to the aid of those who are in need" (*IIaIIae* Q.66, a.7). It is in this way that St. Paul speaks when he says that we are God's helpers (*I Cor.* 3:9).

The Church has always emphasized to the wealthy their responsibility to share their goods with the poor, following the command of our Lord "...[of] that which remaineth, give alms..." (*Luke* 11:41, cited by Pope Leo XIII in *Rerum novarum*, no.22). Hence St. Basil wrote "If you acknowledge them [your possessions] as coming from God, is He unjust because He apportions them unequally? Why are you rich while another is poor, unless it be that you may have the merit of a good stewardship, and he the reward of patience?" (*Homily on Luke, 12:18,* cited by St. Thomas, *Summa Theol, IIaIIae*, Q.32, art.5, 2nd reply). Leo

XIII described how the Church is "constantly pressing on the rich that most grave precept to give what remains to the poor; and she holds over their heads the divine sentence that unless they succor the needy they will be repaid by eternal torments" *(Quod apostolici,* no.9).

For centuries, the Church provided for the needs of the poor *(CCC,* no.2444). Indeed, it was so from the very beginning, as Pope Leo XIII explains:

> Such was the ardor of brotherly love among the earliest Christians that numbers of those who were better off deprived themselves of their possessions in order to relieve their brethren; whence "neither was there any one needy among them" *(Acts* 4:34). To the order of deacons, instituted for that very purpose, was committed by the Apostles the charge of the daily distributions; and the Apostle Paul, though burdened with the solicitude of all the churches, hesitated not to undertake laborious journeys in order to carry the alms of the faithful to the poorer Christians *(Rerum novarum,* no.24).

Through both diocesan churches and monasteries, the poor received food, clothing, medicine and education. The first schools, hospitals, nursing homes, orphanages and hostels for the homeless were all started in Europe by the Catholic Church.

After the Protestant Reformation and the French Revolution, many of these institutions were taken over by the government. The charitable activity of the Church was either greatly restricted or suppressed. The schools, hospitals and other missions of the Church were reopened under state control. Even with the interference of the State, the Church continues her mission to the poor, although in many countries this is quite difficult.

Because we live in a time when the Church does not control the majority of charitable institutions, we tend to think that this is one of the responsibilities of the government. While it is true that the government should aid people in time of crisis and great need, the regular care for the poor should come from the society in general, especially from the faithful (*CCC*, nos.2446-2447). As John Paul II has taught:

> Charity, realized not only by individuals but also in a joint way by groups and communities, is and will always be necessary. Nothing and no one will be able to substitute for it, not even the multiplicity of institutions and public initiatives forced to give a response to the needs — oftentimes today so serious and widespread — of entire populations (*Christifideles laici*, no.41).

Even in the time of Leo XIII, some people condemned the Church for its charitable work, and wanted to put in its place government programs for the poor. Leo XIII answered that "no human methods will ever supply for the devotion and self-sacrifice of Christian charity. Charity, as a virtue, belongs to the Church; for it is no virtue unless it is drawn from the Sacred Heart of Jesus Christ" (*Rerum novarum,* no.24). In other words, one cannot work for the good of the poor if one cares only for their *bodies*. One must care also for their *souls*. In her mission to the poor, the Church looks not only to their temporal needs, but also to their eternal salvation.

St. Basil (329-379) is a Church Father from the western part of what is now Turkey. After his education in Constantinople and Athens, Basil underwent a profound conversion and entered monastic life. He eventually was ordained to the priesthood, and then the episcopacy of Caesarea in 370. Famous for his care for the poor and strangers, he forcefully preached to the rich concerning their obligation to give to those in need.

St. John Chrysostom (347-407) is also a Church Father, famed for his eloquence, which earned him the name *Chrysostom* or "golden mouth." Known for his holiness and his learning, he was appointed Bishop of Constantinople in 397. He left many writings to the Church, including a number of homilies. He insisted always on the need for the rich to reform their luxurious living and care for the poor: "Not to enable the poor to share in our goods is to steal from them and deprive them of life. The goods we possess are not ours, but theirs" (*Homily on Laza-*
***rus*, 2, 5; *CCC*, n.2446).**

Questions for Review

1) Why is it that men alone of all the animals must divide up land in the form of "private property"?

2) Why do people fall into the error of thinking that people will be happier and better if there is no private property?

3) What three reasons does St. Thomas give for the defense of private property? How do you see his reasons confirmed in your own experience?

4) Why does God allow inequality in possessions? What responsibility do the rich have toward the poor?

5) How has the Church helped the poor through the ages? How did this change?

6) Why is it that government programs can never replace the work of Christian charity?

Lesson Fifteen:
"Economic" Injustice, Theft and Fraud

We have now explained why the natural law allows for property, and how the division of property should benefit both rich and poor. Our civil laws are just when they declare stealing a crime and punish those who take unjustly from others.

Stealing can take many forms (*CCC*, no.2409). One may take another's possession in secret against his will, and this is called *theft*. One may take another's possession openly through threats of harm, and this is *robbery* or *extortion*. One may take something from another through deception, and this is *fraud* (*Summa, IIaIIae* Q.61, a.3). Both divine and civil law condemn all of these.

Of these, robbery is the most grave. As St. Thomas explains, "Robbery not only inflicts a loss on a person in his things, but also conduces to the shame and injury of his person, and this outweighs fraud or guile which belong to theft" (*IIaIIae* Q.66, a.9). While the thief avoids harming people in his unjust pursuit of their property, the robber is willing even to kill for the sake of his gain.

The condemnations for robbery in the Scriptures are harsh. We read in *Isaiah* "For I am the Lord that love judgment, and hate robbery..." (*Is.* 61:8). And in *Ezekiel*, "The people of the land have used oppression, and committed robbery: they afflicted the needy and poor, and they oppressed the stranger by calumny without judgment....And I poured out my indignation upon them, in the fire of my wrath I consumed them: I have rendered their way upon their own head, saith the Lord God" (*Ez.* 22:29, 31).

We cannot limit robbery to the unjust taking of material things by private persons. The leaders of communities and states may also use force to take property, contrary to justice. St. Augustine relates the story of a pirate, who was brought before Alexander the Great: "When the king asked the man what he meant by keeping hostile possession of the sea, he answered with a bold confidence, 'What do you mean by seizing the whole earth? But because I do it with a small ship I am a robber, while you who do it with a great fleet, are called an emperor'" (*City of God,* Book 4, c.4). St. Augustine makes the point that without a respect for justice, "what are kingdoms but great robberies?" (*ibid*).

A state, which does not respect natural justice with regard to property, is indeed nothing more than a "great robbery." It is true that the common good may demand that all of us give up something of our private possessions for the sake of the whole. But when a government takes from its people merely for the benefit of the ruling party or some significant majority, this is a form of robbery. For example, God punished King Ahab for taking the vineyard of his subject Naboth (*III Kgs.* 21:19-29; *IV Kgs.* 10:10 [I *Kgs.* 21; II *Kgs.* 10-*NAB*]). Even kings cannot in justice take the possessions of their subjects for their personal gain.

In modern times, the Socialists and Communists have proposed that the government should abolish private property for the sake of the poor (*CCC*, no.2425). The government would own all the property so that all would be equal. Pope Leo XIII however criticized these proposals precisely because they unjustly deprive both rich and poor of their own possessions:

> Their proposals are so clearly futile for all practical purposes, that if they were carried out the workingman himself would suffer. Moreover they are emphatically unjust, because they would rob the lawful possessor, bring the State into a sphere that is not its own, and cause complete confusion in the community (*Rerum novarum,* no.3).

Many governments, inspired by the principles of Socialism, violated the rights of the Church by seizing her property for themselves. Even religious communities that devoted themselves to the care of the people were not spared. As Leo XIII relates, "In many places the State has laid violent hands on these communities, and committed manifold injustice against them; it has placed them under the civil law, taken away their rights as corporate bodies, and robbed them of their property" (*Rerum novarum,* no.39). In the name of helping the poor, the Socialists would even rob those who served the poor.

When the seventh commandment declares, "Thou shalt not steal," it teaches both individuals and governments to respect the just possession of property within a community. And we must remember that, while the Church defends private ownership, she also exhorts those who have in abundance to voluntarily share of that abundance for the sake of the common good (*CCC*, no.2403).

Communism is the belief that man is his own god, and must reorder society that everyone might find his heaven on earth. As a means to this, communism believes in the State ownership of all property so that all social classes will be eliminated, and people will share all things in common. Since the writing of the *Communist Manifesto* (1848) by Karl Marx and Friedrich Engels, a number of nations have adopted communist governments, all with the same results: millions of innocent people tortured, imprisoned or killed; widespread shortages of food and basic necessities; and in general, vastly greater injustices than the ones communism proposed to correct. Although communism no longer exists in Russia and Eastern Europe, it continues in China, Cuba, Vietnam and North Korea.

Questions for Review

1) What are the different forms of economic injustice?

2) Why is robbery a greater sin than theft?

3) How does the story of Alexander the Great and the pirate show that governments are capable of breaking the seventh commandment? How do governments fail to respect private property?

4) What are the errors of the Socialists and Communists about property? How did they treat the property of the Church?

Lesson Sixteen:
Just Wage

As a consequence of the seventh commandment, employers must pay their employees a just wage (*CCC*, no.2434). God commanded His people to pay a just wage to their servants, and threatened them with grave punishments if they failed to do so:

> Thou shalt not refuse the hire of the needy, and the poor, whether he be thy brother, or a stranger that dwelleth with thee in the land, and is within thy gates: But thou shalt pay him the price of his labour the same day, before the going down of the sun, because he is poor, and with it maintaineth his life: lest he cry against thee to the Lord, and it be reputed to thee for a sin (*Deut.* 24:14-15).

This teaching is repeated in the New Testament, for Jesus tells His disciples "...the labourer is worthy of his hire" (*Luke* 10:7). Further, we read in the *Epistle of James,* "Behold the hire of the labourers who have reaped down your fields, which by fraud has been kept back by you, crieth: and the cry of them hath entered into the ears of the Lord of Sabaoth" (*James* 5:4). Commenting on this passage, Pope Leo XIII declared:

> Rich men and masters should remember this — that to exercise pressure for the sake of gain upon the indigent and destitute, and to make one's profit out of the need of another, is condemned by all laws, human and divine. To defraud any

one of wages that are his due is a crime which cries to the avenging anger of heaven (*Rerum novarum,* no.17).

How do we determine if a wage is just? Some might say that a wage is just if both parties agree to the wage. This certainly can be a *sign* that a wage is just, but mutual agreement does not by itself mean that the wage is just.

Pope Pius XI gives three points to be considered in determining a just wage.

1) First, the wage paid to the workingman must be sufficient for the support of himself and of his family. A just wage then must allow "every head of a family to earn as much as, according to his station in life, is necessary for himself, his wife, and for the rearing of his children" (*Casti connubii,* no.117).

We live in a time where it is common for mothers to work outside the home. Before World War II, this was uncommon. It was already starting in Pius XI's time, and he considered it a grave injustice that economic conditions forced mothers out of the home:

> Mothers will above all devote their work to the home and the things connected with it; intolerable, and to be opposed with all Our strength, is the abuse whereby mothers of families, because of the insufficiency of the father's salary, are forced to engage in gainful occupations outside the domes-

tic walls to the neglect of their own proper cares and duties, particularly the education of their children (*Quadragesimo anno,* no.71).

Before we dismiss Pope Pius's statement as "old fashioned," we should remind ourselves that he is not criticizing the custom of working *women,* but working *mothers.* Children, especially young children, need the love and care that only a mother can give them. This is part of our nature, and does not change with the times. In our society, if mothers do not raise their own children, they are given to paid services such as "daycare." Daycare workers, however, no matter how caring or professional they might be, can never love children as a mother does. That is why John Paul II in our own time has written:

> The true advancement of women requires that labor should be structured in such a way that women do not have to pay for their advancement by abandoning what is specific to them and at the expense of the family, in which women as mothers have an irreplaceable role (*Laborem exercens,* no.92).

2) The second consideration in determining a just wage is the condition of the business itself. While the employer cannot increase his profits to the harm of the employee and his family, neither can the employee seek a wage that would be harmful to the business. As Pius XI puts it, "it is unjust to demand wages so high that an employer cannot pay them without ruin, and without consequent distress amongst the working peoples themselves" (*QA,* no.17).

This can be the very practical problem that arises by setting a "minimum wage" enforced by the law. Over time, such a policy can eliminate jobs because businesses that have a tight budget cannot afford to pay employees the minimum wage. For example, suppose a small business can only afford to pay $16.00 an hour for wages, and hires four employees at $4.00 an hour. If the minimum wage is raised from $4.00 to $5.00, the business must lay off one of the employees to keep its payroll at $15.00. While three employees are making a higher salary, one of them must look for another job.

One must also consider the circumstance of a business with regard to the state or country. One cannot for example compare the wages of workers in America to those in the Philippines, and judge the latter as "unjust" merely because it is lower. One must compare cost of living, value of the currency, and many other social factors before one can make a judgment about the differences in salaries between regions or nations.

3) The third condition for determining a just wage is the demands of the common good. Employers must look not only to their private good, but also to the public good upon which their business depends. "The wage-scale must be regulated with a view to the economic welfare of the whole people." When the working man receives a wage that allows him, not only to take care of his family, but also to save little by little until he can buy some property, this benefits the society as a whole. Leo XIII describes three advantages that come by this widespread ownership of land (*RN*, no.47):

1) <u>Social harmony</u> - If working people can be encouraged to look forward to obtaining a share in the land, the result will be that the gulf between vast wealth and deep poverty will be bridged over, and the two orders will be brought nearer together.

2) <u>Widespread prosperity</u> - Another consequence will be the great abundance of the fruits of the earth. Men always work harder and more readily when they work on that which is their own; no, they learn to love the very soil which yields in response to the labor of their hands, not only food to eat, but an abundance of the good things for themselves and those that are dear to them. It is evident how such a spirit of willing labor would add to the produce of the earth and to the wealth of the community.

3) <u>A decrease in the need for immigration</u> - A third advantage still would arise from the fact that men would cling to the country in which they were born; for no one would exchange his country for a foreign land if his own afforded him the means of living a tolerable and happy life.

Many factors go into determining whether a wage is just, and we have touched only on the most fundamental. The Popes themselves always speak of a just wage with regard to the good of the family, because the family is so important for the good of society. A society is composed more of families than individuals. Yet, the principles that the Popes have taught would apply to single people insofar as they too must receive enough to pay for their necessities according to their state in life.

Leo XIII was elected pope in 1878 at 68 years of age, and was expected to rule for a short time as a "transitional" pope. Instead, he reigned for twenty-five years until his death in 1903. He addressed a number of social problems in his encyclical letters during that time, applying the traditional teaching of the Church to the modern world. He condemned the state takeover of Catholic schools (*Militantis ecclesiae*), the state invention of "civil" marriage and legalization of divorce (*Arcanum*), and perhaps most famously, the state repression of worker associations (*Rerum novarum*). Pope Leo was a tireless critic of secular liberalism and socialism. He insisted on the need for governments to recognize God as the source of their just powers (*Humanum genus, Diuturnum illud, Immortale Dei*) and consecrated the human race to the Sacred Heart in 1900 (*Annum sacrum*).

Questions for Review

1) What does the Bible teach about defrauding the working man of his wages?

2) What does Pope Leo XIII teach about a "just wage"?

3) Briefly, what are the three considerations relevant to determining a just wage?

4) What is a "family wage"? Why is it important that mothers stay home with their children?

5) What can limit a business from paying a just wage?

6) How does the common good pertain to a just wage?

Lesson Seventeen:
Truth and the Common Good

In the eighth commandment, God forbids all lying and deception: "Thou shalt not bear false witness against thy neighbour" (*Ex.* 20:16). While many people can invent reasons why it is necessary for them to lie, nobody wishes to be *told* lies. Perhaps we should consider the evil of lying, not from our usual perspective that calculates the need to deceive to save us from some trouble or inconvenience, but rather from the perspective of the person deceived. How can we trust those who lie to us? And how can we be friends with those we do not trust? All societies depend on people being able to trust one another — for assistance, for financial dealings, for basic fairness and decency (*CCC*, no.2469).

As St. Thomas explains, "Since man is a social animal, one man naturally owes another whatever is necessary for the preservation of human society. Now it would be impossible for men to live together, unless they believed one another, as declaring the truth one to another. Hence the virtue of truth does, in a manner, regard something as being due" (*IIaIIae,* Q.109, a.3, 1st reply). Imagine the problems that society would have if no one could trust another for ordinary help and information, if everyone lied to one another regularly and without hesitation.

Our common humanity demands that we will the good for each other, and this means that we owe each other the truth. Blessed Pope John XXIII observed that "All men, therefore, private citizens as well as government officials, must love the truth sincerely if they are to attain that peace and harmony on which depends all real prosperity, public and private" (*Ad Petri cathedram,* no.21).

As followers of Jesus Christ, we have a special regard for the truth, for Jesus Christ is "the way, and the truth, and the life" (*John* 14:6). He is the Truth insofar as He shares in the Divine Nature. In honoring the truth above all, we honor God as well (*CCC*, no.2466). That is why Scripture speaks in such strong condemnation of lying, and with such reverence of the truth.

David says to God, "Thou hatest all the workers of iniquity: Thou wilt destroy all that speak a lie" (*Ps.* 5:7). The *Book of Proverbs* teaches, "Lying lips are an abomination to the Lord: but they that deal faithfully, please him" (*Prov.* 12:22) and "A false witness shall not be unpunished: and he that speaketh lies, shall not escape" (*Prov.* 19:5). The wisdom of *Ecclesiasticus* (*Sirach*) advises, "Be not willing to make any manner of lie: for the custom thereof is not good" (*Ecclus.* 7:14 [*Sir.-NAB*]).

In the New Testament, we learn that the Devil is called the Father of Lies (*John* 8:44). St. Paul teaches the Christians at Ephesus, "Doing the truth in charity, we may in all things grow up in him who is the head, even Christ" (*Eph.* 4:15). In light of this, he counsels them, "Putting away lying, speak ye the truth every man with his neighbour; for we are members one of another" (*Eph.* 4:25).

Our own age struggles with keeping the eighth commandment, not only because it demands bravery and a love of neighbor to tell the truth, but also because we have lost sense of the importance, even the existence of the truth. As Blessed Pope John XXIII lamented, "All the evils which poison men and nations and trouble so many hearts have a single cause and a single source: ignorance of the truth — and at times even more than ignorance, a contempt for truth and a reckless rejection of it" (*Ad Petri cathedram,* no.6).

All societies are nourished by common goods, that is, goods that all can share in, that do not diminish when they are divided. For example, all societies need peace. Peace is a common good, because all can share in it — it is not "my peace" or "your peace." It does not diminish when it is shared. Rather, the more people who share in the peace, the more abundant is the peace, e.g., there is more peace when a country is at peace than when only a city or state is at peace.

Likewise, the truth is a common good. My having the truth does not take from you having the truth. It only increases those who know the truth. The truth is a good in which all can share, and does not diminish the more people share in it.

Many in our age deny that truth is a common good. Instead, we think of truth as a private good, as something that belongs to each man for himself. Thus, for instance, we will speak of "what is true for him" or "what is true for her" instead of what is true for us all. The belief that truth varies totally from person to person is what we call "relativism," as if truth were not absolutely so, but relative to the individual or some set of individuals.

Why would we deny truths that are common to us all? Certainly, some deny absolute truth because they believe it limits their free choice. Truth does limit freedom, but this is hardly an unjust limitation. The truths we learn from medicine help prevent us from poisoning ourselves. These truths help us to live in a healthy way. When our free choice acts for those things that perfect us and make us better, this is the purpose of free choice.

Perhaps more numerous are those who believe we must deny universal truths in order to live with each other peacefully. That is, if I think certain actions are wrong and immoral, and you think they are good, we cannot live at peace. I will despise you, and you will resent me. Only by agreeing that I have my moral "values" and you have different moral "values" can we live at peace. We must not judge each other's beliefs. This view, called ethical or moral "relativism," usually carries pleasant sounding labels such as "tolerance" and "diversity" and "openness."

Moral relativism however is the real threat to peace, not the belief in moral truths. If in fact there is no true morality for all of us, what prevents the strong from oppressing the weak, the majority from taking advantage of the minority, and the rich from robbing the poor? Moral relativism destroys the virtues of justice and generosity. It destroys tolerance, because it destroys the moral obligation we have to bear some evil for the sake of a greater good. As Blessed Pope John XXIII observed, "If we reject this truth, whether out of foolishness, neglect, or malice, we turn our backs on the highest good itself and on the very norm for right living" (*Ad Petri cathedram,* no.7). Indeed, "the very foundations of truth, goodness, and civilization are endangered" (*ibid,* no.8).

More recently, Pope John Paul II has explained:

> If there is no transcendent truth, in obedience to which a person achieves his full identity, then there is no sure principle for guaranteeing just relations between people. Their self-interest as a class, group or nation would inevitably set them in opposition to one another. If one does not acknowledge transcendent truth, then the force of power takes over, and each person tends to make full use of the means at his disposal in order to impose his own interests or his own opinion, with no regard for the rights of others (*Centesimus annus,* no.44).

As Our Lord observed, it is not absolute truth that enslaves, rather, "...the truth shall make you free" (*John* 8:32). The good of our society depends on the love of the truth, and our willingness to tell the truth, no matter what the cost to ourselves. The alternative to the love of the truth is a disordered love of self against the common good.

> When freedom, out of a desire to emancipate itself from all forms of tradition and authority, shuts out even the most obvious evidence of an objective and universal truth, which is the foundation of personal and social life, then the person ends up by no longer taking as the sole and indisputable point of reference for his own choices the truth about good and evil, but only his subjective and changeable opinion or,

indeed, his selfish interest and whim (*Evangelium vitae,* no.19).

Bl. John XXIII became Pope in 1958 at the age of 77. Despite a short reign of five years, Pope John convened the Second Vatican Ecumenical Council, and wrote several encyclicals addressing the social concerns of the age. His first encyclical *Ad Petri cathedram* shows how all human rights find their foundation in human nature given to them by Almighty God. His encyclical *Mater et magistra* honors the 70th anniversary of Leo XIII's *Rerum novarum,* and updates its teaching to the problems of the later twentieth century. His encyclical *Pacem in terris* shows how fidelity to God and the moral law is necessary for international peace.

Questions for Review

1) Why should we consider lying from the point of view of the one being lied to?

2) Why is truth-telling necessary in society?

3) Why do we as Christians have a special regard for the truth?

4) Why does our own age have such a hard time respecting the eighth commandment?

5) How is truth a "common good"?

6) Why do people make the error of thinking truth is a "private good"?

7) Why are moral relativism and other forms of denying universal truth dangerous to society?

Lesson Eighteen:
Censorship and Freedom of Expression

In the ninth commandment, we are told, "Thou shalt not covet thy neighbour's...wife" (*Ex.* 20:17). Jesus perfected this commandment when He taught "...whosoever shall look on a woman to lust after her, hath already committed adultery with her in his heart" (*Matt.* 5:28). In other words, what is shameful to *do* is also shameful to *desire.* Our fallen nature may make these desires difficult to conquer; hence, we need the virtue of modesty to help us guard our words and our actions so that we may be faithful to the sixth commandment (*CCC,* no.2521).

The virtue of modesty is named from "moderation," because it allows us to moderate or measure what we say and do with regard to sexual matters. It tells us that we should avoid speaking obscenely. St. Paul commanded the faithful to avoid "obscenity or foolish talking or scurrility, which is to no purpose" (*Eph.* 5:4) and all "filthy speech out of your mouth" (*Col.* 3:8). Neither should we listen to shameless talk or watch others acting immodestly.

While we are personally responsible for what we say or hear, society also bears responsibility for promoting modesty through custom and law. Some of that responsibility is borne by the bishops, some of it is borne by civil authorities, and some of it is borne by the ordinary people of the community. The precise responsibility of each will vary from time to time, and from society to society. But all must contribute in some way to protection of modesty (*CCC*, no.2525). If not, the society offers little aid to those who struggle against their own weaknesses. At worst, it actively corrupts them, contrary to the common good.

The gravest assaults on modesty usually come through the medium of entertainment. This is not to say that entertainment is bad. Storytelling and other such recreations are a natural part of human life, delighting the passions and the imagination. But storytelling and other artistic representations must respect the moral law. They should not represent wrongdoing in a way that makes it appealing and attractive, destroying our natural sense of shame. Rather, good stories should delight the emotions and imagination, helping the soul to love good things.

Among the early Christians, the theatre was forbidden. The pagan theatre often showed obscene stories and ridiculed Christians and Christian belief ("Theatre," *Catholic Encyclopedia*). In the Middle Ages, after Christianity had conquered paganism, Christians developed their own dramas and theatres. This helps us to understand that entertainment can be good when it supports faith and morals; but it can also be bad, so bad that Christians must avoid public entertainments.

The invention of radio, motion pictures and television has increased the entertainments that are available to people of all classes. And while these media allow for good stories and beautiful artwork, they also allow for obscenity and immodesty. As in every area of social life, the moral law too must judge the arts. Pope Pius XII declared: "If these arts, without fixed laws or moral safeguards, set out on a headlong and unimpeded course, they will certainly become a threat to real culture and a menace to sound morals" (*Miranda prorsus,* no.38).

Some people try to downplay the influence of television and movies, saying that people are not affected by what they watch. That is hardly believable, considering the millions of dollars that are spent every year on advertising. In fact, people are very influenced by what they watch. When they watch bad shows, they are drawn to evil (*CCC,* no.2523). As Pope Pius XI observed:

> All men know how much harm is done by bad films; they sing the praises of lust and desire, and at the same time provide occasions of sin; they seduce the young from the right path; they present life in a false light; they obscure and weaken the wise counsels of attaining perfection; they destroy pure love, the sanctity of matrimony and the intimate needs of family life. They seek moreover to inculcate prejudiced and false opinions among individuals, classes of society and the different nations and peoples. (*Vigilanti cura,* no.20).

Pope John Paul II, addressing the problems that television offers today's society, said the following:

> Television can also harm family life: by propagating degrading values and models of behavior; by broadcasting pornography and graphic depictions of brutal violence; by inculcating moral relativism and religious skepticism; by spreading distorted, manipulative accounts of news events and current issues; by carrying exploitative advertising that appeals to base instincts, and by glorifying false visions of

life that obstruct the realization of mutual respect, of justice and of peace (*Message for World Communications Day,* May 15, 1994).

One cannot defend the harm that obscene and immoral stories cause simply by invoking "freedom of speech." The freedom to destroy family life and marital fidelity is the freedom to destroy society itself, which of course no society can allow (*CCC,* no.2526). Pius XII raised and answered this objection nearly fifty years ago when he wrote:

We cannot approve the stand of those who claim and defend their freedom to depict and display whatever they please, despite the perfectly evident fact that great harm has come to souls in days past as a result of this attitude. For here the issue is not real freedom, which We have discussed above, but unchecked license to express oneself without regard for prudence, even though this be contrary to sound morals and liable to result in serious danger for souls (*MP,* no.32).

Society has many ways of enforcing standards of modesty in its entertainment. The first is the responsibility of ordinary people to avoid shows that undermine the moral law through the glorification of vice. Our own country provides a clear example of this. At the beginning of the 1930s, the American movie industry started to make films that were offensive to faith and morals. Although the movie producers at one point promised not to make such movies, their pledge came to nothing.

As a response to the immoral and irreligious movies that started to appear, the Catholic Bishops mobilized their flock, and formed the Legion of Decency. In the words of Pope Pius XI, "Millions of Catholics of the United States of America, willingly accepting the obligation proposed by the 'Legion of Decency,' promised that they would patronize no cinema entertainment which offended Christian morals and the right precepts of life" (*VC,* no.11).

Other religious groups such as the Jews and Protestant Christians offered their support to the campaign. Faced with this enormous social pressure, the movie industry was prevented from making movies that offended morality or religion. From the early thirties to the late sixties, the Legion of Decency acted as a kind of censor on the movie industry, a censor that did not prevent Hollywood from producing truly entertaining and classic movies (cf. *VC,* no.13).

While ordinary citizens have their responsibility, government also must help promote modest entertainment through its enforcement of laws against pornography and obscene forms of expression. Pope Pius XII explained: "Public authorities are bound, beyond all doubt, to oversee carefully these new means of communication. They should look on this matter not from a political point of view alone, but from that of public morals, whose sure foundation rests on the natural law" (*MP,* no.35).

Elsewhere, Pius XII laid out specific responsibilities for the civil authorities:

This vigilance and care on the part of public authorities is fully justified by their right to protect our civil and moral heritage, and it manifests itself in various forms: censoring of films by state and church authorities and, if necessary, prohibiting them; lists of films published by duly chosen, examining commissions, which rate them, according to their merits, for the information and guidance of the public (*Address to the Society of Movie Producers,* June 21, 1955).

Often our democratic customs make us fear any regulations that restrict free speech. We must remember that the common good is more important than any form of personal freedom. When a people becomes degraded through sexual immorality, the society loses the spirit of self-sacrifice that allows it to continue. For indeed, no society can last that allows the freedom to harm others. We do not for example defend false advertising by "freedom of speech." Likewise, we cannot allow "free expression" that destroys the virtues of modesty and fidelity.

The Legion of Decency began in 1934 and was discontinued in 1971. It worked under the direction of the Bishops of the United States to address the problem of movies that were immoral or irreligious. The Catholic faithful took a pledge every year not to see movies that the Legion of Decency had judged objectionable. As strange as it sounds to us today, movies in the early 1930s experimented with nudity, violence and anti-religious themes. With the pressure from Catholics, and the cooperation of Protestants and Jews, Hollywood was forced to clean up its productions. This allowed them to make the classic movies that many still admire. Other groups today are taking up the challenge against immorality in the media.

Questions for Review

1) Why should we guard our thoughts from evil desires?

2) What is the virtue of modesty? Who bears the responsibility for promoting and protecting it?

3) What distinguishes good kinds of entertainment from bad? Why did the first Christians avoid the theatre?

4) Why have the Popes of the 20th century been so concerned about immoral entertainments?

5) Why are obscene or immoral forms of entertainment not protected by freedom of speech?

6) What responsibility do we have as lay people to help promote and protect good forms of entertainment? How did Catholics fulfill this responsibility in America?

7) What responsibility does government have for promoting modest entertainment?

Lesson Nineteen:
Greed and Envy

In the tenth commandment, we are forbidden to covet our neighbor's property: "Thou shalt not covet thy neighbour's house; neither shalt thou desire his wife, nor his servant, nor his handmaid, nor his ox, nor his ass, nor any thing that is his" (*Ex.* 20:17, cf. *Deut.* 5:21). Our Lord perfected this commandment when He told His disciples, "Lay not up to yourselves treasures on earth: where the rust, and moth consume, and where thieves break through and steal. But lay up to yourselves treasures in heaven: where neither the rust nor moth doth consume, and where thieves do not break through, nor steal. For where thy treasure is, there is thy heart also" (*Matt.* 6:19-21).

When we put our happiness in material goods, we give occasion to two vices in our soul. The first is *avarice* or *greed*. Avarice can be defined as the immoderate or excessive love of possessing (*CCC*, no.2536): "A covetous man shall not be satisfied with money: and he that loveth riches shall reap no fruit from them" (*Eccl.* 5:9). This does not mean that if one has many possessions, one is by that fact avaricious; some people are both very wealthy and very holy. It means that one's desire for them is excessive, and anybody, no matter how much or how little he actually has, can desire to possess in an excessive way. Hence, in *Letter to the Hebrews* we read, "Let your manners be without covetousness, contented with such things as you have" (*Heb.* 13:5).

The second vice caused by putting our happiness in material possessions is *envy*. For, when we see others who possess what we want, we are saddened (*CCC*, no.2539). Hence, envy, according to St. John Damascene, can be defined as "sorrow for another's good" (*On the Orthodox Faith*, Book 2, 14). Instead of rejoicing at the good fortune of another, the envious person is sad, and grows to hate the person who has more than he. Indeed, it is the sin of the devil: "...By the envy of the devil, death came into the world" (*Wis.* 2:24).

Certainly, it is fitting to be sad when others receive good things through evil means, e.g., through theft or fraud. But it is sinful to hate others simply because they have more when they acquired their possessions through entirely just means. St. Paul counsels the Galatians, "Let us not be made desirous of vain glory, provoking one another, envying one another" (*Gal.* 5:26).

When a society ceases to put its happiness in spiritual goods, and in its place puts material goods, the society breaks up into warring classes. Pope Benedict XV described Europe at the beginning of the First World War in light of St. Paul's teaching: "...The desire of money is the root of all evils" (*1 Tim.* 6:10), saying that "If any one considers the evils under which human society is at present laboring, they will all be seen to spring from this root" (*Ad beatissimi apostolorum,* no.14). As Pope Benedict explains:

> There has been instilled into the minds of men that most pernicious error that man must not hope for a state of eternal happiness; but that it is here, here below, that he is to be happy in the enjoyment of wealth and honor and pleasure:

And as these goods are not equally divided amongst men...the envy of the unfortunate is inflamed against the more fortunate. Thus the struggle of one class of citizen against another bursts forth, the one trying by every means to obtain and to take what they want to have, the other endeavoring to hold and to increase what they possess (*ABA,* no.15).

When a society rejects spiritual goods for the sake of material ones conflict is inevitable. Those who have wealth seek to increase it without limit. Hence in the words of Pope Pius XI, "the inordinate desire for possessions, concupiscence of the eyes (cf. *1 John* 2:16) inevitably turns into class warfare and into social egotism" (*Ubi arcano,* no.24). Later, in *Quadragesimo anno,* he declared "The sordid love of wealth...is the shame and great sin of our age" (*QA,* no.136). If Pius XI could say this in 1931, how much more true is it now!

On the other hand, those who seek to gain unlimited power through the government encourage the lower classes to envy. For example, "the Socialists, working on the poor man's envy of the rich, maintain that private possessions of goods should be overturned, and that individual possessions should become the common property of all, to be administered by the State or by municipal bodies" (Leo XIII, *Rerum novarum,* no.3).

Pope Pius XI, in condemning the tactics of the Communists, explains how "[t]he poor are obviously more exposed than others to the wiles of agitators who, taking advantage of their extreme need, kindle their hearts to envy of the rich and urge them to seize by force what fortune seems to have denied them unjustly" (*Divini Redemptoris,* no.61). Whether Socialist, Communist or otherwise, the results of the instigators are the same: "within one and the same nation, within the same city there rages the burning envy of class against class" (Benedict XV, *Ad beatissimi apostolorum,* no.7).

Greed and envy are great causes of social unrest, both within a society and between societies. Pope Leo XIII does not hesitate to name these as causes of war: "Nothing is better suited than Christian virtue, and especially justice, to repress ambition, avarice, and envy which are the chief causes of war" (*Praeclara gratulationis,* no.34). Blessed Pope John XXIII also related these vices to war when he lamented: "Why…do we act as though we are foes and enemies? Why do we envy one another? Why do we stir up hatred? Why do we ready lethal weapons for use against our brothers?" (*Ad Petri cathedram,* no.27).

Peace then comes primarily through a love for spiritual goods over material goods. Only by a love of God, which then overflows into the love of neighbor for the sake of God, will the wealthy share of their abundance with the needy, and those who have less acquire patience and humility in their suffering. As Pius XI explains:

> If the desire for worldly possessions were kept within bounds and the place of honor in our affections given to the things of the spirit, which place undoubtedly they deserve, the peace of Christ would follow immediately, to which would be joined in a natural and happy union, as it were, a higher regard for the value and dignity of human life (*Ubi arcano,* no.38).

St. Katharine Drexel grew up in a wealthy family in Philadelphia, and inherited the family fortune at age 25 on the death of her parents. While visiting Rome, she asked Pope Leo XIII to what religious order she could give her money for missionary work among black people and Indians in America. Pope Leo XIII told her to start one herself. In 1891, she founded the Sisters of Blessed Sacrament for Indians and Colored People, and over the years built many missions, convents and schools, including Xavier University in New Orleans, which is the only black Catholic university in the United States. She was canonized in 2000.

Questions for Review

1) How does Our Lord perfect the Old Testament commandment about covetousness?

2) What is the vice of avarice? Is someone greedy just because he is rich?

3) What is envy? Is it ever right to be sad at the good fortune of others?

4) What happens to a society when its members put all their happiness in material goods?

5) How is a society wounded by greed? How is a society wounded by envy?

6) How are greed and envy causes of conflict between societies? How are greed and envy cured?

Conclusion:

The City of God and the Common Good

We have now reached the end of our study of the social teaching of the Roman Catholic Church. You have no doubt noticed many teachings of the Church that contradict the common opinions of today's society. You have also noticed that the customs and actions to which the Church calls us are very difficult and often rarely practiced. Above all, the hardest teaching to accept (for it is the principal of all the other teachings) is that our society cannot survive without openly honoring Jesus Christ as the King of Nations, and following the directions of His Catholic Church.

And yet, wherever we see the teaching of the Church rejected, people are miserable. When marriages cannot hold together, when the poor are oppressed and disregarded, when life itself is no longer respected or defended, we know that God's law has been set aside. In its place, man has "made up" his own rules.

At bottom, man falls into the error of thinking that he can be happy without God, that he can be his own "god." But our happiness does not come from within; it comes from outside. It comes from the goods that we seek that perfect our nature: love, friendship, knowledge and virtue. No one could consider himself happy if he were loveless, friendless, foolish and cowardly.

Above all other goods, the ones that most perfect man are common goods. These are goods that he shares with others, ones that do not diminish upon being shared. The more man seeks pleasure, money and other such things, the more he is doomed to be unhappy, for these things diminish when shared. That is why they are the source of quarrels and disagreements. But the more a man seeks peace, truth and other common goods, the more he can share them with others with no lessening to himself. Indeed, the more people share in a common good such as the truth, the more truth abounds.

St. Thomas teaches that by nature, we should love the common good more than our own good. Indeed, the social virtues of justice and charity demand at times that we sacrifice ourselves for the common good. "For we observe that the part naturally exposes itself in order to safeguard the whole; as, for instance, the hand is without deliberation exposed to the blow for the whole body's safety" (*Ia,* Q.60, a.5). By instinct, animals sacrifice themselves for the good of their offspring, which in turn provides for the common good of the species.

By our free choice, we should act for the good of our families and communities, even when it demands that we make some sacrifice. A family in which the members act for the common good of the family will be happy, and each member of the family shares in the happiness. On the other hand, a family where each member acts only for his private good cannot be happy.

What is true of the family is also true of the community and the country. As St. Thomas explains, "Each part naturally loves the common good of the whole more than its own particular good....It may be seen in civic virtues whereby sometimes the citizens suffer damage even to their own property and persons for the sake of the common good" (*IIaIIae,* Q.26, a.3). While it may seem that the brave man is unhappy because he risks his life for the community, in fact it is the coward who should be pitied. How can a man be happy who lacks the courage to defend those he loves?

By nature then we should seek the common good, recognizing that our own good is fulfilled in it. Through the grace of baptism, we are able to join the larger community of the Church. We often think of the Church as being a "part" of nations or a "part" of humanity, as if it were part of a larger community. But in fact the Catholic Church is the more universal community, including as it does not only its members on earth, but also all the souls in Purgatory and the blessed in Heaven. Further, the Church is a means for attaining the most universal common good, God Himself. As St. Thomas explains:

> Since God is the universal good, and under this good both man and angel and all creatures are comprised, because every creature in regard to its entire being naturally belongs to God, it follows that from natural love angel and man alike love God before themselves and with a greater love (*Ia* Q.60, a.5).

As we saw earlier, the social virtues allow us to prefer the common good of the city and the country over our private good. The virtue of charity also directs us to the common good, but to the most universal common good. Just as man finds his earthly perfection in the common goods that he can attain by nature, so then does he attain his ultimate perfection by sharing in the most universal common good. St. Thomas reasons from this likeness that:

> Therefore man ought, out of charity, to love God, Who is the common good of all, more than himself: since happiness is in God as in the universal and fountain principle of all who are able to have a share of that happiness (*IIaIIae,* Q.26, a.3).

The whole world of rational creatures is divided on exactly this matter, namely, whether God is to be loved first of all, or whether the self is to be loved first of all. St. Augustine described this division in his book *The City of God.* He distinguished the "City of God," the heavenly city, from the "City of Man," that is, the earthly city. The two cities are not separated by distance, but by love.

> Accordingly, two cities have been formed by two loves: the earthly [city] by the love of self, even to the contempt of God; the heavenly [city] by the love of God, even to the contempt of self....In the one, the princes and the nations it subdues are ruled by the love of ruling; in the other, the princes and the subjects serve one another in love, the latter obeying, while the former take thought for all (*City of God,* 14,28).

In rebelling against God, Satan refused to submit himself to the common good. Instead of finding his perfection in God, the most universal good, Satan desired to find his ultimate happiness in his own power. This is the sin of pride, that is, the sin of desiring one's own excellence in an excessive and disordered way. And it is this pride, this rejection of the common good that separates the good angels from the bad. As St. Augustine explains:

> While some steadfastly continued in that which was the common good of all, namely, in God Himself, and in His eternity, truth, and love; others, being enamored rather of their own power, as if they could be their own good, lapsed to this private good (*City of God*, 12,1).

The rejection of the common good is nothing short of diabolic! And when we fail to act for the common good, certainly we commit the sin of pride. Charity demands that we act for the love of God first above all, in whom we find our good as well. Second, it demands that we love our neighbor as ourselves. Love means to will the good for another, and charity demands that we help our neighbor to share in the common good as well (*CCC*, no.1889). Even when we help our neighbor with material goods, this is a means for the common good, for peace and social harmony.

Further, we look not only to their worldly good, but also to their ultimate good. Thus, charity requires that we look to our neighbor's eternal salvation, which allows him to share in the superabundance of God's goodness (*CCC*, no.1886). As Blessed Pope John XXIII taught:

Men however composed as they are of bodies and immortal souls, can never in this mortal life succeed in satisfying all their needs or in attaining perfect happiness. Therefore the common good is to be procured by such ways and means which are not only not detrimental to man's eternal salvation but which positively contribute to it (*Pacem in terris,* no.59).

The social teaching of the Catholic Church is a beautiful and harmonious whole. It directs the social life of man for this life and the next. For heaven too has its own social order. The blessed dwell in a city founded on the goodness of God Himself. Let us always remember in our work for the good of society, that we are not only called to be citizens of our nation, but that in virtue of our baptism, we are citizens of heaven (*Phil.* 3:20).

Guardian angels not only protect individuals, but also communities and nations. The *Book of Daniel* refers to the "prince of the kingdom of the Persians," which Church Fathers such as St. Gregory the Great interpret to mean the guardian angels of the nation. The *Book of Daniel* also makes reference to St. Michael, who is the guardian angel of the Church. The three children to whom Our Lady appeared at Fatima were taught prayers by the guardian angel of Portugal. This helps us see that God's providence oversees communities as well as persons.

Questions for Review

1) Why is it that a society is doomed to unhappiness once it rejects Catholic social teaching?

2) Why is it that man cannot make himself happy without the help of others?

3) Why do common goods contribute the most to human happiness?

4) How do we know that common goods are more important than private goods?

5) Why is it an error to think that the Catholic Church is part of a larger human society?

6) What is the virtue of charity? How is it related to the common good?

7) What distinguishes the "City of God" from the "City of Man"?

8) Why is it that in helping man to the common good, society should also be helping man to his salvation?

Glossary

Abortion

The murder of an unborn child, 25, 56, 77, 82, 89

Authority

The quality by which persons or institutions make laws and give orders to men and expect obedience from them, 9, 15, 18, 21, 33, 41, 42, 47, 48, 49, 50, 51, 52, 53, 55, 56, 58, 60, 61, 62, 65, 67, 69, 70, 117

Blasphemy

Speech, thoughts, or actions involving contempt for God, the Church, as well as persons or things dedicated to God, 30, 34

Censorship

The supervision of any media (books, movies, etc.) by lawful authority in order to prevent any abuse of it, 120, 124

Charity

A theological virtue exercised by loving God above all things for His own sake, and our neighbor as ourselves for the love of God, 90, 98, 100, 114, 135, 136, 137, 138, 140

Christ, Social Kingship of

The infusion of the Christian spirit into the mentality, customs, laws and structures of society, such that man acknowledges God as king of creation and all humanity not only individually, but socially, 13, 15, 16, 77

Doctors of the Church

Teachers of theology whose writings have provided instruction for the whole Church, 8, 9, 63

Envy

Feelings of sadness at seeing others possess what we want, 95, 128, 129, 130, 131, 133

Euthanasia

The murder of a sickly person, usually through medical means, 25, 56

Fathers of the Church

The first teachers in the Church after the Apostles, who instructed the faithful during her infancy and first growth, 8, 9, 39, 69, 99, 139

Good

That which is desired for its use, pleasure or ability to perfect us in some way, 2, 3, 4, 6, 31, 32, 35, 36, 38, 46, 49, 54, 71, 72, 74, 87, 90, 94, 98, 109, 110, 113, 116, 117, 119, 129, 133, 135, 136, 137, 138, 139

Good, common

A good that can be shared in by many, and does not diminish when it is divided, 2, 3, 6, 26, 31, 48, 49, 51, 57, 58, 59, 61, 62, 65, 67, 69, 71, 72, 90, 91, 102, 104, 109, 112, 115, 117, 119, 121, 125, 135, 136, 137, 138, 139, 140

Greed

The excessive desire for material goods, 128, 131, 133

Infanticide

The murder of a child, 56

The murder of a newborn child, 56

Justice

The virtue by which each gives to others what is due to them, 10, 14, 25, 30, 31, 33, 43, 44, 55, 88, 102, 116, 123, 131, 135

Justice, distributive

The virtue by which those in authority distribute goods to individuals on behalf of the common good, 44

Justice, natural

The standard by which actions are judged as just, based on human nature, 41, 42, 43, 94, 102

Justice, social

The virtue by which each person acts as he should for the common good of society, 10

Liberalism

The view that governments derive their authority from man alone and not from God, 51, 77, 111

Mass, Sacrifice of the

The re-presentation, under the appearance of bread and wine, of Our Lord's sacrifice on the cross, 16, 20, 23, 24, 25, 26, 28, 37, 91

Modesty

The virtue by which we protect purity through speech, dress, and our exterior movements, 120, 121, 123, 125, 127

Moral Relativism

The view that each person should have his own standard of right and wrong, 116, 119, 122

Murder

The unjust taking of innocent life, 11, 51, 55, 57, 59, 60

Obedience

Following the direction of a due authority, 2, 5, 16, 18, 20, 33, 42, 47, 51, 53, 117

Property, private

That which is owned by a private person, and is under his control within the limits of the civil law, 87, 88, 94, 95, 100, 101, 102, 103, 104, 105, 109, 128, 130, 136

Right (political)

A claim that one can make upon others, which they have a duty to fulfill, 1, 2, 5, 6, 17, 31, 39, 43, 46, 58, 61, 64, 67, 68, 117, 125.

Robbery

The taking of another's goods by violence or the threat of violence, 101, 102, 105

Wage, Just

A wage sufficient to allow a working-man to take care of his family in a moderate way, 106, 107, 108, 109, 110, 112

War, Just

A war, declared by due authority for a just cause, and fought with only the violence necessary for victory, 66, 67, 68, 69, 70

Acknowledgments and Documents Cited

Every effort has been made to secure permission for use of published works cited here. Many are in the public domain.

Major Addresses of Pius XII, edited by Vincent A. Yzermans, Vol. I and 2, North Central Publishing Co., St. Paul, Minnesota, 1961.

National Center for Health Statistics

"Spain's Catholic Schools Feel Demographic Decline,"January 17, 2001, www.zenit.org

"Sunday," *Catholic Encyclopedia,* www.newadvent.com

"The Theatre," *Catholic Encyclopedia,* www.newadvent.com

United Nations Department of Economic and Social Affairs-Population Department

Holy Scripture

Citations from Holy Scripture are taken from the Douay-Rheims translation of the *Bible*. Passages having different book titles and numeration in the *New American Bible* are noted in brackets within the citation.

Catholic Bible 3.0, © Catholic Software, P.O. Box 1914, Murray, KY 42071. Used with permission.

Catechism of the Catholic Church

Citations from *Catechism of the Catholic Church*, are from the second edition, Latin text, 1994, 1997, Libreria Editrice Vaticana, Citta del Vaticano; English text 1994, 1997, United States Catholic Conference, Inc., Washington, D.C.

Church Fathers & Doctors

Citations from the Church Fathers are from *A Select Library of the Nicene and Post-Nicene Fathers of the Christian Church*, T & T Clark, Edinburgh; reprinted by W. B. Eerdmans, Grand Rapids, Michigan, 1988-1993. Text on the CD-Rom, *A Catholic Library*, by Catholic Software, Murray, Kentucky. Used with permission.

City of God, St. Augustine: see citation for Church Fathers

Book IV Commentary on the Four Books of Sentences, Book IV, St. Thomas Aquinas, from *Scriptum Super Sententiis Magistri Peter Lombardi*, edited by Maria Fabianus Moos, P. Lethielleux, Paris, 1929-1947. Passage translation by Arthur Hippler.

Summa Theologiae (Theologica), St. Thomas Aquinas, translated by the Fathers of the English Dominican Province, published by Christian Classics, Westminster, Maryland, 1981. Used with permission of Thomas More Publications.

Politics, Aristotle, as found in *Summa Theologiae* (IIaIIae, Q. 64, art.1); see citation for *Summa.*

Papal Encyclicals

All citations from translations available at http://www.ewtn.com document library.

Gregory XVI (1831-1846):

Mirari vos (On Liberalism), 1832

Singulari nos (On the Errors of Lammenais) 1834

Pius IX (1846-1878)

Quanta cura (Condemning Certain Errors) 1864

Syllabus of Errors (1864)

Leo XIII (1878-1903):

Annum sacrum (On Consecration to the Sacred Heart), 1899

Arcanum (Christian Marriage), 1893

Diuturnum illud (On Government Authority), 1881

Humanum genus (On Freemasonry and Naturalism), 1884

Immortale Dei (On the Christian Constitution of States), 1885

Libertas (On the Nature of True Liberty),1888

Militantis ecclesiae (On St. Peter Canisius) 1897

Mirae caritatis (On the Holy Eucharist), 1902

Praeclara gratulationis (The Reunion of Christendom), 1894

Quod apostolici (On Socialism, Communism and Nihilism), 1878

Rerum novarum (On the Condition of the Working Classes), 1891

Benedict XV (1914-1922) World War I

Ad beatissimi apostolorum (Appealing for Peace), 1914

Pius XI (1922-1939)

Casti connubii (On Christian Marriage), 1930

Divini Illius Magistri (On Christian Education), 1929

Divini Redemptoris (On Atheistic Communism), 1937

Mit brennander sorge (On the Church and the German Reich) 1937

Non abbiamo bisogno (On Catholic Action in Italy), 1931

Quadragesimo anno (The Reconstruction of the Social Order), 1931

Quas primas (On the Feast of Christ the King), 1925

Ubi arcano (Peace of Christ in the Kingdom of Christ), 1922

Vigilanti cura (On Motion Pictures), 1936

Pius XII (1939-1958) World War II

Address to the Society of Movie Producers, 1955.

Al particolare ("Speech to Farm Owners and Operators"), 1946

Christmas Address of 1942 "The Internal Order of States and People"

Christmas Address of 1944 "True and False Democracy"

Christmas Address of 1956 "Communism and Democracy"

Ci torna ("The Movies and the Nature of Man"), 1955

De premier ("The Moral Limits of Medical Research"), 1952

Miranda prorsus (On the Communications Field), 1957

Summi pontificatus (On the Unity of Human Society), 1939

Blessed John XXIII (1958-1963)

Ad Petri cathedram (On Truth, Unity and Peace), 1959

Mater et magistra(Christianity and Social Progress), 1961

Pacem in terris (Peace on Earth), 1963

Paul VI (1963-1978)

Evangelii nuntiandi (Evangelization in the Modern World), 1975

Humanae vitae (On Human Life), 1968

Mysterium fidei (On the Holy Eucharist), 1965

Populorum progressio (On the Development of Peoples), 1967

John Paul II (1978-2005)

Centesimus annus (100 Years Later), 1991

Christifideles laici (On the laity), 1988

Evangelium vitae (The Gospel of Life), 1995

Gratissimam sane (Letter to Families), 1994

Familiaris consortio (On the Family), 1981

Laborem exercens (On Human Work), 1981

Message for World Communications Day, 1994

Novo millennio ineunte (At the Beginning of the Third Millennium) 2001

Sollicitudo rei socialis (On the Social Teaching of the Church), 1987

Veritatis splendor (The Splendor of the Truth), 1993

Conciliar Documents

All citations from translations available at www.ewtn.com document library.

Second Vatican Council

Dignitatis humanae (Declaration on Religious Liberty), 1965

Gaudium et spes (Pastoral Constitution on the Church in the Modern World), 1965

Gravissimum educationis (Declaration on Christian Education), 1965

List of Illustrations

Cover: *Last Judgment* by Fra Angelico, Museo di S. Marco, Florence, Italy. Photo credit: Scala/Art Resource, NY. Used with permission.

Page 5: *John Henry Cardinal Newman*, from a painting by W.W. Ouless, etching by P.-A. Rajon. Reprinted from *The Catholic Encyclopedia*, Volume X, facing p.800, © 1911 by the Robert Appleton Co., New York.

Page 11: *Moses* by Michelangelo. Reprinted from *The Catholic Encyclopedia*, Volume X, facing p.596, © 1911 by the Robert Appleton Co., New York.

Page 18: Blessed Miguel Pro. Photo courtesy of Ann Ball.

Page 27: Pope Pius X. Reprinted with permission © Servizio Fotografico *L'Osservatore Romano*, Vatican City.

Page 33: Pope Gregory XVI, from a photo of his tomb in St. Peter's Basilica. Reprinted from *The Catholic Encyclopedia*, Volume VII, p.8, © 1911 by the Robert Appleton Co., New York.

Page 39: St. Justin, Martyr, © Rev. Michael Busch; from the website of St. Justin Martyr Church, Unionville, Ontario (www.stjustin.com). Used with permission.

Page 47: Pope Benedict XV. Reprinted with permission © Servizio Fotografico *L'Osservatore Romano*, Vatican City.

Page 52: Blessed Pius IX. Reprinted from *The Catholic Encyclopedia*, Volume XII, facing p. 136, © 1911 by the Robert Appleton Co., New York.

Page 58:   Pope John Paul II. Reprinted with permission © Servizio Fotografico *L'Osservatore Romano*, Vatican City.

Page 63:   St. Thomas Aquinas, from an engraving in *Oprac.Zywoty. Swietych*, by Dr. A. Marschewke. Reprinted from *1998 Illustrated Saints Calendar and Daily Planner*, © 1997, Catholic Truth Society. Courtesy of TAN Books & Publishers, Rockford, Ill.

Page 69:   *St. Augustine* by Botticelli. Reprinted from *The Catholic Encyclopedia*, Volume II, facing p.100, © 1911 by the Robert Appleton Co., New York.

Page 77:   Pope Pius XI. Reprinted with permission © Servizio Fotografico *L'Osservatore Romano*, Vatican City.

Page 84:   Pope Paul VI. Reprinted with permission © Servizio Fotografico *L'Osservatore Romano*, Vatican City.

Page   91:   Saints   Isidore   and   Maria.   From www.ncrlc.com/isidoreandmaria.html, © National Catholic Rural Life Conference. Used with permission.

Page 99:   *St. Basil*, from *The Meaning of Icons*, Leonid Ouspensky and Vladimir Lossky, page 123, © 1952, 1982 St. Vladimir's Seminary Press (575 Scarsdale Rd., Crestwood, NY 10707). Used with permission.

Page 99:   *St. John Chrysostom*, from an engraving in *Oprac. Zywoty. Swietych*, by Dr. A. Marschewke. Reprinted from *1998 Illustrated Saints Calendar and Daily Planner*, © 1997, Catholic Truth Society. Courtesy of TAN Books & Publishers, Rockford, Ill.

Page 104: Russian labor camp from the online exhibition at www.osa.ceu.hu/gulag/b.htm Photo reprinted from *Letters From Russian Prisons*, International Committee for Political Prisoners, edited by Alexander Berkman, © 1925, Boni, New

York. Hyperion Press (Westport, Connecticut) edition published in 1977.

Page 111: Pope Leo XIII. Reprinted with permission © Servizio Fotografico *L'Osservatore Romano*, Vatican City.

Page 118: Blessed John XXIII. Reprinted with permission © Servizio Fotografico *L'Osservatore Romano*, Vatican City.

Page 125: Anti-blasphemy protest. Reprinted from America Needs Fatima website: www.tfp.org/anf/anti_blasphemy/corpus.htm. Used with permission.

Page 132: St. Katharine Drexel. Reprinted with permission from the Archives of the Sisters of the Blessed Sacrament, Bensalem Pennsylvania.

Page 139: *St. Michael the Archangel*, © Matthew Brooks, Hubbardston, Massachusetts. Used with permission. See website www.net1plus.com/users/artcatholic.